The

Ascending
Lifestyle

The
Ascending
Lifestyle

living in heaven

while walking on earth

Dan Luehrs

Foreword by Wade Taylor

TATE PUBLISHING
AND ENTERPRISES, LLC

Published by Tate Publishing & Enterprises, LLC
127 E. Trade Center Terrace | Mustang, Oklahoma 73064 USA
1.888.361.9473 | www.tatepublishing.com

Tate Publishing is committed to excellence in the publishing industry. The company reflects the philosophy established by the founders, based on Psalm 68:11,
"The Lord gave the word and great was the company of those who published it."

Book design copyright © 2012 by Tate Publishing, LLC. All rights reserved.
Cover design by Blake Brasor
Interior design by Christina Hicks

Published in the United States of America

ISBN: 978-1-61346-640-7
1. Religion / General
2. Religion / Christian Growth / Spiritual Growth
11.10.27

I dedicate this book to my long-time friend Vinnie Bauldree, who survived the bombing attacks from the Nazis army in England. You have been a tremendous blessing to me over the years. If you came only to America to encourage me, I thank God for bringing you here. I pray that God would abundantly reward you with His likeness throughout eternity.

Thank you!

Table of Contents

Foreword

There are many prophetic messages being given today, but there is one clarion call that has been going out since the days of John the Revelator, which is "Come up here!"

Dan Luehrs has heard this voice, and he has seen and heard a present word for the body of Christ to ascend into the realms of God and receive strength and truth for our day.

We can know present truth through our experiencing the *The Ascending Lifestyle*. We can rise above the levels of fear, hopelessness, depression, addictions, and other controlling spirits. These intend to manipulate and keep us captive in the earthly realm, when God has His glorious presence and strength waiting and available for us in the heavenly realms.

If we will take the time each day to draw near to the tangible presence of God, He promises to draw near to us and dine with us in the garden of our heart, and manifest Himself to us on a daily basis.

We are about to come into the most intense times of human history and will need to know how to ascend into the Spirit realm of God. Unless we know how to ascend and receive the grace of God daily, we will not make it through the times that are upon us.

This book, *The Ascending Lifestyle*, will help us to understand the importance of spending quality time with God, and to rise above the temporal earthly events that seek to steal our eternal victory that Jesus has already paid for us.

He, the great Overcomer, lives in us, so we cannot fail because it is impossible for God to fail! God has called us to be the overcomers that will ascend over all that is put in our path, so we can ascend to the throne of God to sit with Jesus, forever and ever!

—Wade E Taylor.

Dan Luehrs

The Ascending Lifestyle

> If ye then be risen with Christ, seek those things which are above, where Christ sitteth on the right hand of God.
>
> Colossians 3:1 (KJV)

God has given you the right in Jesus Christ to seek and find eternal riches (truths) from above, where He is, to keep them in your heart as your very own for all eternity. The riches of heaven are far above earthly treasures, which perish. As Christians, we are (have been) raised up with Jesus into the realm of the spirit world where He sits in His throne on high. Most Christians are waiting to die to go to heaven for this to happen, but I want to show you from the Word of God that you can have heaven here and now. It is God's desire *for His will to be done in earth as it is in heaven*; this is why we pray the Lord's prayer. Now we must start believing and experiencing it in everyday life.

Heaven is touching the earth, and the veil between them is getting thinner by the day until one day, the kingdom of God is going to manifest clearly before all people and there will be no denying its power and glory for King Jesus will be seen by all the inhabitance of the earth. But before that can take place, Jesus will be seen in and through His people, and those with the eyes of their understanding opened will be able to see Him in each other. What makes heaven, heaven is the Lord's presence, and His presence is what makes for good relationships. Heaven is about relationship. A relationship with our heavenly Father first and foremost, and then with all those who are in heaven we will have great relationships with because there will be no sin found there to destroy them. We crave relationships with our spouses, children, family, and friends, for we must have these to maintain a healthy mental and spiritual life.

Within a few weeks I have met three Christian women that have changed my life for good. Even though we did not know each other after the flesh, we somehow knew each other by the spirit. The Bible tells us in 2 Corinthians 5:16, "Therefore from now on we recognize no man according to the flesh; even though we have known Christ according to the flesh, yet now we know Him thus no longer." None of us have held Jesus' hand in the flesh, but yet each of us has sensed His presence guiding and helping us at times in our life. Once when I was in my office, Jesus sat opposite from me and began to speak to me, and I said to Him, "Why can I not see you with my natural eyes?"

He replied, "Because you can see me with the eyes of your understanding."

I then thought of Ephesians 1:17–18:

> That the God of our Lord Jesus Christ, the Father of glory, may give to you a spirit of wisdom and of revelation in the knowledge of Him. I pray that the eyes of your heart may be enlightened, so that you may know

Dan Luehrs

what is the hope of His calling, what are the riches of the glory of His inheritance in the saints.

Notice that the riches and the glory of God are in His people, and God wants us to see Him in each Christian. We have to see Jesus with our heart, or we will not see Him at all. John 3:3 says, "Jesus answered and said to him, 'Truly, truly, I say to you, unless one is born again, he cannot see the kingdom of God.'" In other words, we cannot see King Jesus until we are saved. Now please hear me carefully; Jesus wants us to see Him in each other. Can you imagine what would happen to the body of Christ if we could truly see Him in one another? Well, we would honor each other with such respect that the world would stand up and notice that we really love each other for who we are. We will fulfill the new commandment as we see Him in each other.

> A new commandment I give to you, that you love one another, even as I have loved you, that you also love one another. By this all men will know that you are My disciples, if you have love for one another.
>
> John 13:34–35, NAS

Think of how this will change marriages, families, churches, and the entire world. Truly, heaven will have come down to earth.

I was in California on vacation, and my rental car was late, so I decided to look over the downtown area of Modesto. I went into an ice-cream shop and began to talk to the owner of the store, and she said something about the Lord and then introduced me to her mom who was eighty years old. I took one look at her and noticed something about her that got my curiosity going, and I said to her that I somehow knew her. I spent the next three and half hours in their shop talking about the Lord with them and the whole next day. As I sat across the table from her in an Italian restaurant, I asked her, "How could it be that we know each other so well?" It was like we had known each other all our lives.

A few weeks later, once again, I met a Christian lady, and we talked for five hours about the Lord. As we sat down in a restaurant, I could feel the Lord's presence greatly there like He put a bubble of His presence around us to reveal Himself. This has happened to me only once or twice in my life with other people. I was intrigued with this lady; it was as if I could see into her heart, and what I saw there was amazing. She had such depth in the Lord. She, like the other ladies, had gone through such horrendous situations, and yet they stayed faithful unto God. I was seeing this in their hearts, and I was amazed at the glory of the Lord that I beheld.

That whole week I thought of the time I had with her and what I saw in her, so I asked the Lord, "What did I see in her?"

He then said, "Me."

I knew that was right because in each of these ladies their familiar spirit was the Lord. The Lord is now revealing Himself in and through His people as never before and is having us make connections with other Christians so that He might manifest His kingdom through us. In Rick Joyner's "Word for the Week," he writes:

> With all of the focus on the outward signs, many are missing the most important one of all—what is taking place right in our midst. There is something so remarkable going on in the church, and few, even in the church, seem to be seeing it. There is a mighty army such as the world has never seen before, or will see again, starting to come together. What we should be looking for more than anything else is for the Lord to come forth in His people.
>
> The way we know that someone is called as a teacher is not by their knowledge, degrees, or how articulate they are, but by seeing the Teacher in them. Likewise, the way we know that someone is a true pastor is not

Dan Luehrs

by their certificates or even their compassion for people, but when we see our Shepherd in them. The way I know that someone is called to leadership in the church is when I see my King coming forth in them. We only have true spiritual authority by abiding in the King.

The Lord really is starting to come forth in His people. We are seeing true teachers, shepherds, pastors, prophets, and I believe soon, true last-day apostles, some of whom are among us now. As I shared last week, we will see even the feeble in the body of Christ rise up as mighty warriors like David. We are going to see the great men and women of God who were raised up throughout church history like seeds, with a thousand like Martin Luther, a thousand like John Calvin, a thousand like John Knox, a thousand like John Wesley, a thousand like Zinzendorf, and a thousand like Billy Graham, and so on. These were all seeds and we are going to see the harvest at the end of the age. However, the greatest of all is to see Jesus coming forth in His people.

That is just what God wants us to see in others: Jesus. He is easier to see in some because of their relationship with Him. Some spend more time with Him than others, and the more you hang around someone, the more you become like them. We must stop seeing so much of the negative in others and getting hung up on everything that is wrong with them when we have the same things wrong with ourselves. If we focus on the negative, we will see it; but if we ask the Lord to help us see Him in others, I believe that we will see Him and be dazzled. The Lord of glory has chosen to abide in their heart. So if He has received them into His kingdom, how much more should we? God is truly doing a new work in the earth so let us not find ourselves opposing Him in others even if they are from another part of town or other denominations that we do not agree with. It is imperative that we start looking for the Lord in His people for us to get to where we need to go because we are all a part of the great temple that God is building in the spirit realm. "In whom the whole building, being fitted together is growing into a holy temple in the Lord" (Ephesians 2:21, NAS). Jesus is now manifesting Himself in and through His people; we should be excited to seek for Him in all of our relationships. Seek Him who is from above.

Being Raised up in Him

> Having been buried with Him in baptism, in which you were also raised up with Him through faith in the working of God, who raised Him from the dead.
>
> Colossians 2:12 (NAS)

> And raised us up with Him, and seated us with Him in the heavenly places, in Christ Jesus.
>
> Ephesians 2:6 (NAS)

According to these two verses, we have been raised from the dead and are seated with Jesus in the realm of the spirit where He is now. I do not always feel like I am seated with Him in the heavens. Matter of fact, this world feels more demonic at times than it does heavenly.

Notice what Colossians 2:12 says: "Through faith in the working of God ..." There we have it. Through faith we *have been* and *are* raised up into the realm of the spirit with Him. While we are living in a natural body, God wants us to have a spiritual experience with Him in His realm each day. God has invited us into His realm, for it is our home, so why not take the time to come to Him each and every day? He is our daily bread, and He is our drink that satisfies our spirit man; if we do not take time daily to be with Him, we will just shrivel up and die spiritually.

> No one has ascended to heaven but He who came down from heaven, that is, the Son of Man who is in heaven.
>
> John 3:13 (NKJV)

Dan Luehrs

When Jesus was on earth, He was able to be in heaven and on earth at the same time because His spirit was connected to the Father, and so are we: "That they all may be one, as you, Father, are in me, and I in you; that they also may be one in us, that the world may believe that you sent me" (John 17:21, NKJV). We can ascend in and through Jesus anytime we desire to by seeking heavenly things. Your spirit man is able to soar into the heavens with God because your spirit is already connected to God. That makes your spirit as large as heaven itself. When I am connected to the Internet, I am connected to the World Wide Web and can get whatever I need; and when I am connected to God with my spirit, I am connected to *unfathomable riches* in Christ Jesus. Whatever you need from heaven, like truth, grace, healing, peace, wisdom, etc., God is there to give it to you by your asking and taking by faith. If all things come from God who is spirit, why should it be so difficult for us to believe God for anything natural or spiritual because it all comes out of Him?

I want to bring this a little further. What you and I really need to be seeking from above is *life*—God's life every day: "For you have died and your life is hidden with Christ in God" (Colossians 3:3, NAS). I once thought my life to be lived on earth is somehow hidden in Christ and that I needed to find it, but now I understand what life is, it is the power of God like a current of electricity that gives power to this life at all times. Because without God's life flowing into us daily, we can get depressed and try to find life through many different forms to get an adrenaline high going in the natural so that we might feel alive. We can get high from another person, drugs, alcohol, sex, or something that gets our interest for a short time, but then we begin to look elsewhere until we get our next high. Colossians 3:3, in the Interlinear Bible, reads: " ... And the life of you has been hidden with Christ in God." This is my interpretation, "Your energy, joy, and purpose for living is all found in Jesus if you will seek and find Him each and every day." This is how we are to overcome in this lifetime because we have His life flowing through us at all times as we stay connected to the vine.

People use many different avenues to get a high in life. Most think of drugs and alcohol that get people high, but the truth of the matter is anything that gets our adrenaline going is a high, and we can get addicted to it quickly. I believe that God's life is the most addicting substance in the universe, but very few people know how to obtain it. Seeking the things above is the true and original high designed by God. The problem is, most people will not pay the price to come up to Him daily to get it; they will not lay down their life of sin and pleasure to receive it because the price is too high. But they will pay the price and put down the money to get false highs for a short time from the world because it feels good to the natural senses, but their spirit man is left empty. They go from mountaintop-to-mountaintop experiences.

Before Jesus came into our hearts, we lived on one plain: the natural. It was totally earthly with natural goals and aspirations because that is all we could see and understand. But now we have come to Christ and have been enlightened, for He has opened our spiritual understanding to see that we have a spiritual side to us that needs to be taken care of. To understand this, think of a cell phone and how it works with no wire or cables tying you down. You cannot see the microwaves that the phone is working on, but be sure they are there because you are talking on the phone. Even if you have a good phone but do not have it activated, the microwaves in the air will do you no good because the phone is not programmed. The same is true with our spirit man and the spirit realm where God is. He has always been there, but our spirit man has not always been activated through faith in Jesus to live in the realm of heaven. Once we come to Jesus, we are brought to life, and then our spirit man can communicate with God in prayer and begin to learn His Word and live by faith in the manifest presence of God. It's a wonderful life. Jesus promises us in John 14:21, "He who has my commandments and keeps them, he it is

Dan Luehrs

who loves me; and he who loves me shall be loved by my Father, and I will love him, and will disclose myself to him." By knowing and obeying God's Word, He promises to reveal Himself to us; what better promise can we have than to have His presence with us? Let us say with Moses, "If thy presence does not go with us, do not lead us up from here" (Exodus 33:15, NAS). Amen.

But of those who do not know Him, the Bible says that they are excluded from the life and presence of God. How terrible is that?

> Being darkened in their understanding, excluded from the life of God, because of the ignorance that is in them, because of the hardness of their heart.
>
> Ephesians 4:18 (NAS)

If you are not practicing the presence of the Lord daily, it is possibly because of three things:

1. You are ignorant of the fact that He is available to you at all times. The Lord asks this question: "Do I not fill the heavens and the earth, declares the LORD?" (Jeremiah 23:24, NAS). If the Lord is everywhere, that means that we can have His presence anywhere.

2. Simply because we are not taking the time to seek His face but have time to seek anything else that might get our attention.

3. Because we have a hardened heart with sin in our life that we do not intend to give up so the presence of the Lord does not penetrate us to convict us because we have said no to the Lord's wooings over and over.

When the Bible tells us that we are seated with Him, why would we not want to sit with Him each and every day? Our being seated with Him is more than us just sitting down in heaven—it means to be seated in a seat of authority, like the county seat or the seat of government. It is on God's mercy seat that we sit down together with Him each and every day.

Being Made Alive by Ascending

Even when we were dead in our transgressions, made us alive together with Christ (by grace you have been saved).

Ephesians 2:5 (NAS)

Life is what God is; it is not just our existence on earth as we think, but it comes from Him alone. To live without Him is to live without true life; this is the reason why people look for life in many different things, but it only brings death in the end. God breathed His life into Adam, but when he sinned, death—or separation—came between him and God, and only through Jesus can we have true life back in us again. When Jesus breathed on to His disciples in John 20:22, He was breathing His life back into man as He did in the beginning with Adam; and now by His Holy Spirit, He has done the same for us if we have asked Jesus to come into our hearts. But not only then, He wants to breathe His life into us every day if we will take the time to be with Him and ask Him to.

There are different forms of life all around us. When I look at my desk, I see matter (steel and other man-made materials) made into a desk or the bookshelves, or what have you. Science tells us that matter is nothing more than a bunch of atoms put together, but what is an atom? One word: *energy*. There is life in an atom; just split one and see what happens—*boom!* The facts are, just a few atoms could kill every person on planet earth. We understand that there is an energy force all around us including in the air with lightning and the pull of the earth's north and south poles and from the moon and the sun, and only God knows what else there

Dan Luehrs

is. And we have not even started to talk about the demonic powers of the air that have influenced man through the ages.

I said all that to say this: the physical body is made of energy, billions and billions of atoms and cells that have life in them. Life must come from somewhere, and that somewhere is Jesus Christ, for He is the life of all things. Jesus is life; He created all things by the power of His Word, and His word gives life to every living thing, and they solely exists for His good pleasure. God's Word, who is Jesus Christ, is power (energy), and His Word brought everything into existence. Read who the Bible claims Jesus to be:

> In Him was life, and the life was the light of men.
>
> John 1:4 (NAS)

> Jesus said to her, "I am the resurrection and the life; he who believes in Me shall live even if he dies."
>
> John 11:25 (NAS)

> Jesus said to him, "I am the way, and the truth, and the life; no one comes to the Father, but through me."
>
> John 14:6 (NAS)

> For just as the Father has life in Himself, even so He gave to the Son also to have life in Himself.
>
> John 5:26 (NAS)

What most of us understand about life is that our heart is beating inside of our chests, and we can see life all around us each day. We get natural life from eating foods that are grown on the earth to maintain physical energy and good health from these foods that we eat so that we can maintain life. No food, no life; it is that simple.

The same is true of our spirit man; when we were saved, we received the life of God in our inner man. But God has made it so that we must come to Him daily to feed our spirit man because life comes from Him and Him alone. Just as the children of Israel had to gather manna each day in the wilderness to live, so we must do likewise in the spirit to receive spiritual food or energy from the Lord. As Christians, the presence of Jesus and His Word have now become our spiritual bread and drink.

> Jesus said to them, "I am the bread of life; he who comes to me shall not hunger, and he who believes in me shall never thirst."
>
> John 6:35 (NAS)

The Father gave the Son life, Jesus is life, and if we want God's life, we must come to the Son every day to receive it. Think of God as an electric power plant. Once I visited a hydroelectric plant on a private tour, and my host said to me, "I want to bring you into the room where the power is being made." As we walked into the door, I could feel the power in the air, and it made me quake from just sensing it. I have felt that same power in the presence of the Lord; this is what God wants to give us: his power to live everyday life. We must come to Him.

Just like a battery in a flashlight, unless the battery has a charge in it, the light will not come on, so it is with Christians that have been regenerated or given life through Jesus Christ. We must abide in Him daily to receive the energy of God to maintain a strong spiritual life and to stay on the path of life. Most Christians will not take the time to do this, and then they wonder why they are so lethargic toward spiritual things. Jesus said in John 15:5, "I am the vine, you are the branches; he who abides in me, and I in him, he bears much fruit; for apart from me you can do nothing." Notice, unless we stay connected to Him daily and continually, we will not have His life flowing in us; we must stay joined to Him as fruit does to a tree, or we will die spiritually. Our spiritual growth process requires that we as a branch receive its life from the vine, and to do so, we must set apart time to be with Jesus for fellowship and communion. We must wait on Him in His presence as a battery waits on a charger so that His life can flow into us and become a personal reality within us. The Lord is calling us to arise and come up into the heavens with Him. Only as we make ourselves available to Him and reject the path of least resistance and begin to walk in the spirit will this be possible.

Most Christians today do not have the joy of the Lord's life as their strength because they do not come to Him daily to receive His presence where there is fullness of joy. Jesus said, "These things I have spoken to you, that my joy may be in you, and that your joy may be made full" (John 15:11, NAS). True lasting joy comes from the Lord's life in us. I don't know about you, but I have not come to the place in my life that I am living full-time in the fullness of His life and joy that He has promised us. "I have come that they may have life, and have it to the full" (John 10:10, NIV). This is how we can rejoice in and through anything because we are receiving our life from Him continually. This is the importance of us ascending daily and learning to receive His life anywhere and anytime that we need to.

I had a dream that I was in a building looking at a stage with a large stockpile of gold and a person said, "Take some." We did; there was no panic as we took the gold into our heart. Then someone asked me for some, so I gave it to them, and they received it into themselves. I felt like we were stealing it, and I was expecting the police to come after us, but they never did. Then in my dream, I met a man, and he said, "I saved some gold for you; I hide it under the grand piano." I then looked, and sure enough, there was a half a bar under each leg, and I awoke.

My interpretation of this is: an angel came to me in January of 2007 and told me that it was now the time of gold, meaning the nature and authority of God. He is now giving His life and nature to His people for the taking, and we must take it into ourselves. The piano means for us to rejoice in God no matter what happens in our life; His gold is hidden in our worship. "Sing to Him a new song; play skillfully with a shout of joy" (Psalms 33:3).

Not long after this, I met a lady that had a similar vision. In her vision, five people were sitting on a gold stage or platform, and the Lord said to them, "Command and decree what I tell you, and it will be done; you have my platform of authority."

Why Two Lives, Anyway?

> For we know that if the earthly tent which is our house is torn down, we have a building from God, a house not made with hands, eternal in the heavens. For indeed in this house we groan, longing to be clothed with our dwelling from heaven; inasmuch as we, having put it on, shall not be found naked.
>
> 2 Corinthians 5:1–3 (NAS)

Have you ever asked yourself why we have to live here in this fallen state of humanity when in fact the Bible teaches us that we have a new and sinless body and life waiting in heaven for us? Why even go through this life of pain and suffering anyway if we are going to have that which is never going to die or decay?

The way I see and understand this natural world and life is that it is only a testing ground to see who will be willing to pay the price to follow the Lord and become like Him in the process. Then when this earthly life is over and we have paid the price to become like God, He will give us true and lasting riches and a place in His kingdom that is eternal and not temporary like on earth.

> So if you have not been trustworthy in handling worldly wealth, who will trust you with true riches? And if you

Dan Luehrs

have not been trustworthy with someone else's property, who will give you property of your own?

Luke 16:11–12 (NIV)

Nothing in this natural world lasts forever, for it all will grow old and fall apart in time and will go back into the ground where it came from, including our bodies. If this be true, why do people spend so much time and effort trying to build wealth and their earthly kingdoms when in fact, they will give it all to someone else when they die? Or why do people spend so much time and money on their physical bodies when they are only going to be dust in a few short years? Because they are spiritually blind and short-sighted to the fact that our time spent on earth is only a testing ground to what we will have and be doing in eternity with God.

Before companies put a product out on the market, they test it in real-life terms and see if it will hold up to the abuse and the environment of the product. For instance, if a product was being made for children, the company would try it out on children to see, first of all, if the children will like it, and if the product will stand up to the abuse that it will receive. But say a company wants to make and sell cars, they would first test them in the real world and then sell them in the marketplace. These companies do not want to sell a defective product that will bankrupt the company in the process. In the end, people would get hurt from the product and the people of the company would lose their jobs, so the final outcome would be worse than the beginning. We, like those products, are being tested to see if we will be faithful.

Knowing that the testing of your faith produces endurance. And let endurance have its perfect result, that you may be perfect and complete, lacking in nothing.

James 1:3–4 (NAS)

Beloved, do not be surprised at the fiery ordeal among you, which comes upon you for your testing, as though some strange thing were happening to you.

1 Peter 4:12–13 (NAS)

In the same way, God has been doing the same thing as companies do with mankind over the ages to see if we will obey and follow Him so that in the end, He can reveal His life in and through us to the nations. There is no greater experience in life than to know life Himself and to have Him live in and through us. God Himself is the power plant of life; God is life. His very existence gives life just as the sun gives life to all that is on the earth, yet all the suns and stars in the universe could not compare to Him because He created them all. Hear this: the power plant of eternity, God, is inviting you into the very core of Himself so that you may have life in you that is eternal.

And this is eternal life, that they may know Thee, the only true God, and Jesus Christ whom Thou hast sent.

John 17:3 (NAS)

Notice that eternal life is not time in of itself. Eternal life is God. It is not that God's life will live for eternity, but that we can know the true eternal life in and through the person of Jesus Christ. By us ascending into the spirit realm with God each day, we are choosing to spend time with Him and getting to know Him through our life experiences that He gives us. As we worship God through the good and bad times of life, we are maturing in the faith and becoming like Him because what we are saying is that we trust Him and honor Him with our life. As we worship, His presence fills our heart with the breath of heaven, and this is what gives us life that we need to maintain a healthy and happy lifestyle.

When we are in His presence, we need to ask God to fill us with the Holy Spirit to the full so that we are saturated with

Dan Luehrs

God. The days that we are living in are evil, and they will suck the very life from us if we let it. We must guard our heart for out of it flows the very issues of life, and once we have His life flowing in and through us, we can give it away to others that are hurting and needy like my dream with the gold. His life can flow through us in many different ways like: our words, our presence, our touch, and through books and writings like this.

To have intimacy with God is to know true life. How we spend our time here will determine our placement in eternity with God, for the closer we are to Him now like He was with Enoch, the closer we will sit next to Him in heaven. My prayer is, "Oh, God, let me be closer to you than any person who ever lived." Ask Him to help you come closer and closer, as the day draws near. I ask you, if we do not want to be close to God now, why would He want us to be close to Him in heaven?

> Then Jesus said to His disciples, "If anyone wishes to come after me, let him deny himself, and take up his cross, and follow me."
>
> Matthew 16:24 (NAS)

I do not see how spending time in God's presence can be a cross, but I do understand that at first it can be to our flesh because we always want to be doing something that makes us feel good. The cross is made for one thing, and that is to kill our carnal nature. Kill your self-nature by spending time with God each and every day.

Many people, including Christians, are stuck in the past when they were hurt. Just because a person has aged in years does not mean that they are mature in their spirit and are becoming like Jesus. They are stuck and hung up spiritually. We must all learn to forgive each other, but if we do not, our present spiritual life will be filled with anger, bitterness, resentment, and the list could go on into lust, greed, and all the other sins of the flesh. God is allowing these things in our lives to mature us like Himself so that we can go higher into other spiritual challenges. This is why we cannot waste our trials by murmuring and complaining. God cannot allow higher spiritual challenges in our lives because He knows that they would only overcome us quickly, and we would give up and quit the good fight of faith.

> Therefore we do not lose heart, but though our outer man is decaying, yet our inner man is being renewed day by day. For momentary, light affliction is producing for us an eternal weight of glory far beyond all comparison, while we look not at the things which are seen, but at the things which are not seen; for the things which are seen are temporal, but the things which are not seen are eternal.
>
> 2 Corinthians 4:16–18 (NAS)

If you knew that what you were going through was preparing you for the throne, would you not be willing to go through it? If you knew that this cup that you were drinking from was from the Lord, would you not drink it? Since we enter the kingdom of God through tribulations and giant pearls (trials and tribulations) are doorways to the kingdom, why not go through them with His grace and strength instead of drudgery?

Unbelievers do not have the life of God in them according to Ephesians 4:18: "Being darkened in their understanding, excluded from the life of God, because of the ignorance that is in them, because of the hardness of their heart." The Bible tells us that we must be careful not to harden our hearts when we are going through trying times, which is easy to do; we can get mad at God when He does not do what we think He should. But when we grow in Him and praise Him through all things, we soon realize that He is fully trustworthy through anything, and we can know that He is allowing the best for us even when its hard, and we have no understanding why God is allowing this in our life.

Dan Luehrs

Who alone possesses immortality and dwells in unapproachable light (fire); whom no man has seen or can see. To Him be honor and eternal dominion. Amen.

1 Timothy 6:16 (NAS)

God alone possess *life* without end, and if we want His life, we must live by His ways and rules according to the Bible. He dwells in a flame of fire that nothing can penetrate, and He is inviting us into Himself; so why not take this opportunity to turn your life over to Him fully and ascend into the heavens with Him now?

Sharers of
His Life

Now if we are children (sons of God), then we are
heirs—heirs of God and co-heirs with Christ, if indeed
we share in his sufferings in order that we may also
share in his glory life.

Romans 8:17 (NIV)

I have heard many single people say, "I would like to find someone to share my *life* with." In essence, what they are saying is, "I
do not want to go through life by myself. I want to experience
this life with someone." Ah, there you have it; life is an adventure
to be journeyed through. I have had the privilege of traveling to
many places in the earth by myself, but when I had seen something really special, I have said to myself, *I wish that my wife could
be here to share this experience with me.* Or I have thought, *When
my wife can come with me someday, we will go here or there because I*

do not want to experience this by myself. God's life is also an experience for us, and in the end, *His life* is all there is. Think of what it means for us to share His life.

> I appeal as a fellow elder, a witness of Christ's sufferings and one who also will share in the glory (life) to be revealed.
>
> 1 Peter 5:1 (NIV)

God wants us to experience His life. The Lord awoke me one night and said, "I have made man to share my life with." There was a strong emphasis on the word *share*.

> He called you to this through our gospel, that you might share in the glory (life) of our Lord Jesus Christ.
>
> 2 Thessalonians 2:14 (NIV)

The glory of the Lord is His life, for the whole *earth* is filled with the glory, or life, of the Lord, and God wants our personal earth (body) to be filled with His life. One of the first astronauts to see the earth from the moon commented on how the whole earth was filled with life, and everywhere else he could see in the whole universe was filled with death. Yet in contrast to that, a Russian cosmonaut stated on his return to earth that he had been in outer space, and he did not see God. Both men pretty much saw the same thing with two different outlooks. Why? One was able to see the life of God in the earth, while the other was totally blind to God because of his perception of what God is. God is life, and there is no death in Him. Everything living in God's creation gets its life from God, including the devil and his hordes.

For some unknown reason, God wants to share His life with us. But why? Is He lonely? Or is it because He is a Creator, and He must be continually creating? Or is it that He just wants

Dan Luehrs

someone to love Him for who He is, and in doing so, God gives him His greatest prize? His life and glory.

When we think about God sharing His life with us, we cannot totally comprehend what this would entail. When I think of life, I think of an electric power plant that gives life to a city and to all its inhabitance. And this is just why God wants to give us His life, to share it with the people of the world.

> In Him was life, and the life was the light of men.
>
> John 1:4

> For just as the Father has life in Himself, even so He gave to the Son also to have life in Himself.
>
> John 5:26

If we are to be co-heirs with Jesus as the sons of God, then we will also be given His life as the Father has life within Himself to restore creation back to its pristine nature that it was created to be in the beginning. With the fall of Adam, all of creation suffered, but with man's restoration, all of God's creation will be restored through man.

The Road to Life

> Terah took his son Abram, his grandson Lot son of Haran, and his daughter-in-law Sarai, the wife of his son Abram, and together they set out from Ur of the Chaldeans to go to Canaan. But when they came to Haran, they settled (stopped) there. Terah lived 205 years, and he died in Haran.
>
> Genesis 11:31–32 (NIV)

According to the above verses, Abraham's *father* was to leave their homeland of the Chaldeans and travel to the land of Canaan to receive it as their inheritance. But Abraham and his father got comfortable in Haran and stayed there rather than moving on to Canaan. His father did not complete the journey to the land of Canaan but ended up dying on the *road* to the promised land. The name *Haran* means "roadway." Haran was to be a resting place for them along the way to the promised land; it was not to be place to live and die. They basically fell asleep in Haran by becoming rich and comfortable with the world and their surroundings. In fact, Abraham did not get the call of God to leave for the land of Canaan until *after* his father died. Abraham was only fulfilling the original call of God that was placed upon his father to leave the land of the Chaldeans and go to Canaan but had gotten side-tracked by staying in Haran too long. Acts 7:2 says, "The God of glory appeared to our father Abraham while he was still in Mesopotamia (Chaldean), before he lived in Haran" (NIV). The way that this verse is written in the New Testament, the translators have translated Genesis 11:31 to mean that Abraham got the call of God to leave their homeland and travel to Canaan rather than his father leading the way there. But it was not until his father died that Abraham was called of God to leave from Haran, *not* from the Ur of the Chaldeans. So I believe that the Greek text of Acts 7:2 should read: "The God of glory appeared to the father of Abraham while he was still in Mesopotamia, before he lived in Haran." According to Genesis, Abraham's father was the leader of their expedition to the land of Canaan, not Abraham.

We are also called of God to go out of our Haran into the promised land of the fullness of God that many of our forefathers in the faith failed to bring us to. They also died in Haran (the roadway), which is the traditions of man, religion, and the fear of man and failure. This has stopped many Christians from fulfilling their call of God upon their lives. Abraham and his father must have greatly feared the giants that were living in the land of Canaan. I can almost hear the people of Haran say to them, "Don't go down to the land of Canaan because there are giants there, and no one ever survives very long there." So they settled for the land of good and plenty of Haran rather than the best land of Canaan. Abraham and his father must have lived in Haran a long time because Genesis 12:5 says that they had "accumulated" a lot of possessions in Haran. In fact, Abraham's father was 205 years old before he died. This tells me that God had given him plenty of time to fulfill his mission in life, but he did not because he would not go to Canaan where he was called to live. I believe that Abraham's father, Terah, was God's first choice to become the "Father of our faith," but because of the fear of the unknown, he did not go on to fulfill his mission in life as many Christians do.

But when Terah died, God finally called Abraham out of Haran to the land of Canaan: "Now the LORD said to Abram, 'Go forth from your country, and from your relatives and from your father's house, to the land which I will show you" (Genesis 12:1). They were in Haran so long that God even called Haran, "Your country." The father of our faith obeyed God at the age of seventy-five to fulfill what his father did not do. This tells me that God does not give up on us when we are getting older to fulfill our mission in life. We may think that we are too old to start something big for God, but even Caleb said to God at the ripe old age of eighty-five, "Give me this mountain." Yet what Abraham didn't know at the time was that through his obedience to God, God was going the send Jesus the Messiah through his bloodline to save all people.

This should make us shudder; our obedience now could make a difference in the lives of many people throughout eternity. This makes me think of all the settlers that came to America to start a new life for themselves by the leading of the Lord. Did they realize that when they left their lives behind in their old countries that they were going to a new land to build a new country that would free millions of people from oppression and injustice throughout the world? Did the hard-working farmers know at the time when they were clearing the land by uprooting trees and picking rocks that this land would one day feed millions of people around the world? I think not. None of us lives to ourselves, and none of us dies to ourselves; our successes and failures will reverberate down throughout eternity. The question is, will we allow God to do His work through us, or will He have to find someone else to finish what He has called us to do?

I believe that God is wanting to do this same thing through many of His people today, but because many Christians will not trust God enough to move on to what He has called them to, they too will simply die on the roadside of life without ever placing a foot in the promised land. The key for us to go on into the fullness of God's life is that we do not quit along the roadside to prosper in the things of the world. For we too could die in Haran instead of traveling on the road to the promised land. And this is just what many people have done. All Christians are on a journey to the Celestial City to be transformed into the likeness of Jesus, but many of His people have gotten their eyes off of Him and back on to the world's way of doing things, thus being sidelined in the ditch on the road to life. It is with great difficulty that we are to stay on the road to His fullness of life, and few are those who obtain it. But those who do will free all of creation from sin and decay into the freedom of the sons of God: "That nature (creation) itself will be set free from its bondage to decay and corruption [and gain an entrance] into the glorious freedom of God's children" (Romans 8:21, AMP). Hallelujah.

It's All a Matter of Choice

Where we are at today in our spiritual growth is because of our choices we have made in the past. And these choices that we make today will determine where we will sit with Jesus on His throne tomorrow. Either we are killing the flesh in us through our obedience, or we are killing the life of Jesus in us by our disobedience. Either our spirit man is growing stronger in us through our tribulations, or the man of sin is growing stronger in us by our neglecting to obey the Son of God. It's one or the other; we cannot have it both ways. Our flesh is being crucified when we obey Jesus, or He is being crucified in us by not serving Him, for he is being crucified afresh in me (Hebrews 6:6, KJV).

When Jesus came into our hearts, it was through the seed of God's Word. It was just a seed. But as we watered and fed that seed in us, it began to grow unto full Sonship, or into the likeness of Jesus. But by our own choosing and neglecting of Him, we can kill the life of Jesus in us so that He is crucified and thirsty in us, even as He died upon His own cross saying, "I thirst." And this is what happens to many Christians by putting Him to an open shame before the Father because they are denying Him spiritual food. The kingdom of the beast (the world system) in us must be brought down so that our desires and thoughts must be only for Jesus and what is best for His kingdom in us. Our flesh must be starved; this happens by God giving us more of a hunger for Jesus than for worldly things. Jesus is a seed in us that must be fed and given drink. Jesus said in Matthew 25:35, "I was thirsty and you gave me drink and I was hungry and you gave me food." Jesus is starving in most Christians today because all they give Him to eat is junk food: worldly entertainment along with worldly and religious head knowledge. Daily we must feed the life of Jesus in us with the milk and meat of His Word, along with a fresh drink from the river of God.

One day, I felt pain in my spirit for sinning against God, and I said to the Lord, "What is this pain?"

He said, "You're killing Jesus."

I began to weep before the Lord for the pain that I was causing Him. I then had a revelation of what these verses mean about us crucifying Jesus afresh or anew; "Wake up, and strengthen the things that remain, which were about to die (the life of Jesus in us); for I have not found your deeds completed in the sight of my God" (Revelation 3:2, NASB). We must not lose our focus on what God has called us to; if we do not quit in the process of following Him, we will win the prize of our high calling in Christ Jesus. We must awaken out of our slumber and sleep and stop hitting the snooze button; it's time to wake up and run the race and fight the good fight of faith. God has given us a wonderful promise in 2 Thessalonians 1:10–11 if we will live worthy of this high calling of Sonship:

> On the day He comes to be glorified in His holy people and to be marveled at among all those who have believed. This includes you, because you believed our testimony (message) to you. With this in mind (our high calling in Him), we constantly pray for you, that our God may count you worthy of his calling, and that by his power he may fulfill every good purpose of yours and every act prompted by your faith.
>
> (NIV)

But how are we to be counted worthy of such glory and honor? Paul tell us in 2 Thessalonians 1:4–5 (NIV):

> Therefore, among God's churches we boast about your perseverance and faith in all the persecutions and trials you are enduring. All this is evidence that God's judgment is right, and as a result you will be counted worthy of the kingdom of God, for which you are suffering.

There we have it; it's through our perseverance, faith, persecutions, and trials that we are enduring. No wonder why we are to glory in our tribulation; our suffering as Christians is not in vain

Dan Luehrs

after all. It is producing for us an eternal weight of glory beyond all comprehension.

The glory that we are to receive at the coming of the Lord is His flame of fire. This is the very *life* and power of God that will be imparted to us to change mankind and all of creation by bringing them into the knowledge and experience of Jesus Christ. We are His messengers of flames of fire that the Lord will reveal Himself through to all mankind and bringing them to judgment: "The Lord Jesus shall be revealed from heaven with His mighty angels (messengers) in flaming fire" (2 Thessalonians 1:7, NASB). Notice that verse 11 is speaking about our *knowing* of being counted worthy of this *calling* (to be the ministers of flames of fire). John the Baptist knew who he was in the Scriptures—a forerunner to Jesus. Jesus knew who He was—the long-awaited Messiah. And we also must find ourselves in the Scripture; we are *called* to be the ministers of flames of fire/life. That is if we are counted worthy of such honor.

God's calling for us is not to bring destruction to mankind with His fire and life, but to be vessels of reconciliation and redemption (Isaiah 63:4, NASB). This is for us to bring all things back to Him in right standing. Notice that God in His own way will repay all those who are troubling us with their *own* tribulation: "Seeing it is a righteous thing with God to recompense tribulation to them that trouble you" (2 Thessalonians 1:6, KJV). These people that are persecuting the church are not getting away with anything, for they too will suffer. I believe what happened to Paul on the road to Damascus is a sign of what will eventually happen to every person on the face of the earth. Paul deserved God's wrath and judgment for killing and persecuting the church, but God, in His riches of mercy, knocked him off his high horse and blinded him with the light of His truth, that Jesus Christ is Lord. Do you see God's mercy being displayed through Paul to all people?

> But for that very reason I was shown mercy so that in me, the worst of sinners, Christ Jesus might display his unlimited patience as an example for those who would believe on Him and receive eternal life.
>
> 1 Timothy 1:16 (NIV)

Then God told Ananias in Acts 9:16, "For I will show him how much he must suffer for my name's sake." Paul then had to go through great suffering to get to where he was in his experience with Jesus. And so will everyone else experience great suffering to enter the kingdom of God (Acts 14:22, AMP). "Through many hardships and tribulations we must enter the kingdom of God" (Acts 14:22, AMP).

The vengeance that people will receive at the coming of the Lord is the great tribulation that all Christians are experiencing when they come to know the Lord and grow in Him: "Who shall be punished with everlasting destruction from the presence of the Lord, and from the glory of his power" (2 Thessalonians 1:9, KJV). In other words, those who do not follow the Lord now will not be able to come into the glory of God until they have paid the price of following Him through their tribulation. Many Christians that are now sitting on the fence of the world will have to go through great tribulation that God prescribes for them, so that they too will die to the man of sin in them for the destruction of the flesh (1 Corinthians 5:5, KJV).

> Our fathers disciplined us for a little while as they thought best; but God disciplines us for our good, that we may share in his holiness.
>
> Hebrews 12:10 (NIV)

Oh, yes, my friend, God has His life awaiting you on Mount Zion to be transformed into His likeness and life. Don't quit now, you're almost there.

Dan Luehrs

Where the Eagles Are Gathered

Eagles are awesome birds in flight, soaring in beauty and grace; they do not have to flap their wings to fly like other birds do to get air born. Oh, no, all they have to do is spread their wings and mount up with the wind to take flight to the currents of air high above the earth. The words *mount up* mean to, "arise, ascend, and to bring up." Eagles build their nests at the highest point they can find so that they can see both food and predators afar, even as much as one mile. They also build their nests up high so they can feel the wind currents to take flight into it. They are so in tune to the air currents that they can ride the wind and soar into the heights above. The stronger the wind, the higher they can fly into the heavens above the storm. Eagles are the kings of all other birds that must fly in the lower heavens and are envied by all. When other birds chase the eagle, all he has to do is go higher and higher into the sun to lose the enemy. That's because eagles can fly straight into sun and not be blinded. We can say that the eagle flies like the wind because he does. There are many more deep truths that I could write about the natural eagle, but that is not my purpose here. My goal is to show you from scripture the truths of where God's eagle saints are called to arise now.

Eagle Saint, Arise

> But those who wait on the Lord shall renew their strength; they shall mount up with wings like eagles, they shall run and not be weary, they shall walk and not faint.
>
> Isaiah 40:31 (NKJV)

The Word of God beckons us as Christians to become like the eagle. If we are told in the Bible to consider the ant's way, how much more should we study the majestic eagle and learn from it? Man studies birds and other flying creatures to see how their aerodynamics work, but we Christians should study the eagle to show us how to soar into the heavens with Jesus where He is seated above.

> If then you were raised with Christ, seek those things, which are above, where Christ is, sitting at the right hand of God. Set your mind on things above, not on things on the earth.
>
> Colossians 3:1–2 (NKJV)

We as eagle saints have already been raised up into the heavens where Christ is seated, so why not seek Him with all our heart? You and I are not called to be like the chicken that pecks around in the dirt and sits under clouds of depression, but we are called to arise above depression, doubt, fear, and the confusion of the enemy. We as eagle saints are called to use the adversity of the

Dan Luehrs

wind in the time of storms of life to cause us to go higher into the realms of glory. The storms of life are the very thing that propels us into the higher realms of glory than what we were in before; we could not get into these realms without the trials.

We must be set free from this earthbound life so that we can mount up into the heavens above all the distractions of the world. When we lose the baggage of sin and the cares of this world, we are free to go higher: "Therefore we also, since we are surrounded by so great a cloud of witnesses, let us lay aside every weight, and the sin which so easily ensnares us, and let us run with endurance the race that is set before us" (Hebrews 12:1, NKJV). We must see that our trials are the very things that we need to go higher. As great pain and sorrow is being released throughout the earth, those who do not know how to soar above it all will suffer greatly. But we who get our strength from the Spirit of God "shall renew their strength" by waiting in the Lord's presence, He will fill us with His glory, and we will go higher than any other generation before. Tribulations are doorways into the kingdom of God, and as greater tribulations are coming on the earth, they will only set us free to go higher in Christ.

The enemy wants to pull us down with the weight of the world and sin so that we cannot fly high into the realms of God. Years ago, I had a dream that I was in a hot air balloon flying into the heavens, and as I was just starting to enjoy the ride and the sights, I was being pulled back down to the earth. I thought, *What is up with that?* When I looked down, there were some demons pulling on the ropes trying to get the balloon into a dark shed so that I could not fly again. Then God said to me, "Cut the ropes." And I awoke. The demon's wanted me in depression so that I could not bring others into the heavens with me.

Our calling is to seek God and to soar into the heavens where our citizenship and strength is in Christ Jesus. There are many hungry Christians that will not settle for the run of the mill religious services but will seek God for all that He has available to this generation. These are eagles saints that are gathering in the heavens above all the mundane Christian lifestyle of today, which is really only pecking around the dust of the earth. The eagles of God will not settle for anything but live, fresh meat from the table of God to satisfy their hunger.

The Eagles Are Gathering

> And they answered and said to Him, "Where, Lord?" So He said to them, "Wherever the body is, there the eagles will be gathered together."
>
> Luke 17:37 (NKJV)

This can be a confusing verse to many because it is in reference to the time of the revealing (or manifestation) of the Lord in His people. We as the church are called to sit in heavenly places now, which is our inheritance in the spirit realm of God. We were made spirit and body, meaning, we can dwell in both places at one time just as Jesus did when He was on earth. "No one has ascended to heaven but He who came down from heaven, that is, the Son of Man who is in heaven" (John 3:13, NKJV). When Jesus was on earth, He was able to be in heaven and on earth at the same time because His spirit was connected to the Father and His body was on earth as we are now.

When we understand the Scriptures and our calling to dwell in the heavens, then we can perceive what Jesus meant when He said, "Wherever the body is, there the eagles will be gathered together." You might say, "How do you know that we are the eagles spoken of here?" Jesus said in Mark 13:27, which is Mark's interpretation of what Jesus was saying about what would happen before His return, "And then He will send His angels, and gather together His elect from the four winds, from the farthest part of earth to the farthest part of heaven." The Lord is gathering His

Dan Luehrs

elect (the body of Christ) to come together in the heavens for the great battle of the end-time. Today, His body is still on earth (the church) along with those in heaven; the body of Christ in heaven is now the great cloud of witnesses that are dwelling with God in the spirit realm.

But we who are called to be eagle saints cannot dwell in the realm of the glorified saints as of yet because we do not have a glorified body as they do. Flesh and blood cannot inherit the kingdom of God; only our spirit man can ascend into the realm of God and receive spiritual strength, which is our daily bread. Isaiah 60:8 (AMP) says, "Who are these who fly like a cloud, and like doves to their windows." The windows of heaven are open now for those who will ascend into the realm of God to breathe the air of heaven, to give them the strength to live for Him each day. "And behold, the heavens were opened to Him" (Matthew 3:16, NKJV). The heavens were opened to Jesus as He was on the earth, and right now, they are opened for us to ascend into the realm of God to gain Christ.

What is happening right now with the eagle saints is this: they are recognizing each other by the spirit and can tell that the person they are talking with has the same lifestyle in the spirit of God and are able to communicate on the same spiritual level of understanding. They are now gathering in the open heavens above all the religious and worldly conversation and works of the flesh, which only bring spiritual death to the hearers. Read below 1 Corinthians 2:12–14 in the Wuest translation to help you understand, that we, who are growing in the spirit of Christ, speak another language than carnal Christians or unbelievers can understand.

> But as for us, not the spirit of the world system did we
> receive but the Spirit who is of God in order that we
> might come to know the things which by God have been
> in grace bestowed upon us, which things also we put

into words, not in words taught by human philosophy but in words taught by the Spirit, fitly joining together Spirit-revealed truths with Spirit-taught words. But the unregenerate man of the highest intellectual attainments does not grant access to the things of the Spirit of God, for to him they are folly, and he is not able to come to know them because they are investigated in a spiritual realm. But the spiritual man investigates indeed all things, but he himself is not being probed by anyone. For who has come to know experientially the Lord's mind, he who will instruct Him? But as for us, Christ's mind we have.

As the glory of God becomes stronger and stronger on the earth, the earth is going to shake as Mount Sinai did when God came down and spoke with Moses: "Now Mount Sinai was completely in smoke, because the Lord descended upon it in fire. Its smoke ascended like the smoke of a furnace, and the whole mountain quaked greatly" (Exodus 19:18, NKJV). It was quite a fearful thing for God's people to see His glory, all the people trembled, as did Moses at the very sight the earth shook at His presence. "Oh, that Thou wouldst rend the heavens and come down, that the mountains might quake at Thy presence" (Isaiah 64:1–2, NAS). But we are not to fear the great shaking taking place around the earth. As the Lord is pouring out His Spirit on the earth, great judgments will be taking place because the Lord is drawing near, but we who know how to ascend in the spirit realm above all the commotion on earth will be kept in perfect peace.

The fourth living creature was like a flying eagle.

Revelation 4:7–8 (NKJV)

This eagle saint was not held to the earth but had the face of a flying eagle to soar above the events taking place on earth. We

Dan Luehrs

who know how to dwell in the heavens and are not earthbound as others are that receives the wrath of the devil because we are receiving our strength and protection from God if we have been trained to go up high in Him.

Satan is not going to take this lying down either. Great wrath will be poured out on the church from his evil hoard as we see in Revelation 12:13: "Now when the dragon saw that he had been cast to the earth, he persecuted the woman who gave birth to the male child." Now read verse 14 and see what God does for His people while the enemy is persecuting them:

> But the woman was given two wings of a great eagle, that she might fly into the wilderness to her place, where she is nourished for a time and times and half a time, from the presence of the serpent.
>
> (NKJV)

After the church has given birth to the man-child (these are the sons of God, see verse 5), Satan will persecute the church greatly, but God will teach those who have ears to hear to come up into the heavens to escape the wrath of the enemy. The Wuest Bible translates Revelation 12:14 this way: "And there was given to the woman the two wings of the great eagle, in order that she might be flying into the uninhabited region into her place." At this point, the devil has been cast down from the heavens, and the spirit realm is uninhabited by the demonic powers, the church can rest in the realm of the spirit to be trained and strengthened for the great battle to come. The great last battle will be when Jesus returns on the white horse with the saints to restore the earth and all the people on it.

Why am I telling you all this? Because if you are not ascending now with the wings of a great eagle, you will be facing more pains of this earthly life then God means for you too. He has made a way of escape; you must wait upon the Lord and renew your strength, spread your wings, and come up into His realm. How do we come up? By spending time in His presence every day and breathing the air of heaven, for it is life to you in these days that we live in.

The Darkness Is Gathering Also

> Do not be deceived, God is not mocked; for whatever a man sows, that he will also reap. For he who sows to his flesh will of the flesh reap corruption, but he who sows to the Spirit will of the Spirit reap everlasting life.
>
> Galatians 6:7–9 (NKJV)

Light and darkness dwell on the earth at all times. When one side of the earth is dark, the other is light; this is the way God has made it in the beginning. The same is true with every person that has ever been born after Adam sinned in the garden. There is darkness in each one of us, and if Jesus lives in you, He is the light of you. God is light, and the devil is darkness; but one day, there will only be light because the kingdom of God is coming down from the Father of light: "The city had no need of the sun or of the moon to shine in it, for the glory of God illuminated it. The Lamb is its light" (Revelation 21:23, NKJV).

The darkness of Isaiah 60:2 is now gathering on earth even as God's glory is being poured out at the same time: "For behold, the darkness shall cover the earth, and deep darkness the people." The darkness I see gathering is great, and if we are not getting our daily bread (life) from Jesus by seeking Him every day and by soaring into the heavens, we will be overcome by darkness. I believe the day is coming, and now is when no person will be able to sit on the fence of Christianity. Either they will be on fire for God, or they will be living for self and a life of sin because that which is planted in their heart will be manifest. The Bible says

Dan Luehrs

that everything sown must be reaped: "For he who sows to his flesh will of the flesh reap corruption" (Galatians 6:8, NKJV). This means that if people have sown seeds of wickedness, they will reap a harvest of evil back into their lives, and the same is true with that of righteousness—they will reap peace and joy. Those who have sown to wickedness and have not repented will come into the full likeness of the devil, and those who have sown unto righteousness will come into the full likeness of Jesus Christ. Which one do you want to be? There are only two choices.

Second Thessalonians 2:9–12 says that Satan is coming with all power. This power is coming in and through his fallen body of people just as Jesus has His body (the church to manifest Himself through). Some people that have been to hell said that it was in the shape of a human body with a heart and all.

> The coming of the lawless one [the man of sin, or the body of Satan in the earth] is according to the working of Satan, with all power, signs, and lying wonders, and with all unrighteous deception among those who perish, because they did not receive the love of the truth, that they might be saved. And for this reason God will send them strong delusion, that they should believe the lie, that they all may be condemned who did not believe the truth but had pleasure in unrighteousness.
>
> And even as they did not like to retain God in their knowledge, God gave them over to a debased mind, to do those things which are not fitting; being filled with all unrighteousness, sexual immorality, wickedness, covetousness, maliciousness; full of envy, murder, strife, deceit, evil-mindedness; they are whisperers, backbiters, haters of God, violent, proud, boasters, inventors of evil things, disobedient to parents, undiscerning, untrustworthy, unloving, unforgiving, unmerciful; who, knowing the righteous judgment of God, that those who

practice such things are deserving of death, not only do the same but also approve of those who practice them.

Romans 1:28–32 (NKJV)

All hell is about to break forth on the earth in darkness, for I have seen it coming for many months now. "The rulers of the darkness of this age" (Ephesians 6:12, NKJV). But God has an army of many sons of glory (light) that is going to overcome the power of the darkness in its entirety, and Satan will be cast into the pit. Darkness cannot overcome light; it is impossible. What night has ever overcome the sunlight? None.

There are two beasts in Revelation 13 that we must know is coming, one of them is already here. One comes out of the sea (which is the people of the world): "Then I stood on the sand of the sea. And I saw a beast rising up out of the sea, having seven heads and ten horns, and on his horns ten crowns, and on his heads a blasphemous name" (Revelation 13:1–2, NKJV). One of the ways that this beast is keeping the people bound to the earth is through the economic system of man rather than trusting Christ to be their provider and Lord.

The second beast that comes out of the earth are the demonic powers that are held for a time when God's great out pouring is taking place in the earth. The devil wants to turn the nations from Christ in the time of a worldwide revival when one billion souls are going to be saved: "Then I saw another beast coming up out of the earth, and he had two horns like a lamb and spoke like a dragon" (Revelation 13:11, NKJV). These powers that are to come are not men or the so-called Antichrist. These are demonic powers that have come to control mankind to make them their slaves to sin and death.

The first beast is from the sea and is now in control of the world system (Babylon). It causes people to live their lives for the vanity of the world rather than Jesus Christ because it blinds people's minds from seeing the light of the glory of Jesus. God's

Dan Luehrs

people are going to be delivered from the beast system that is causing them to live more for the world then for Him. If you find yourself going through financial hardship, it may very well be God preparing you for what is to come so that you might be set free from the system of men.

When God's people are delivered from the first beast, the second beast will come with even greater power that will only reinforce the first beast to enslave the people to the world system. As God is pouring out His Spirit in great measure in the earth, the enemy has to counter it with enslaving people to the world through the love of money. The devil's people will fight against the move of God and His people, but they will lose because the Lord of hosts is coming to lead the battle and win. "And he exercises all the authority of the first beast in his presence, and causes the earth and those who dwell in it to worship the first beast, whose deadly wound was healed" (Revelation 13:12, NKJV). We must be free from this world economic system so that we can go where He sends us and be used of God to deliver others from it.

The deadly wound of the first beast is an economic depression of the likes of 1929 or even much worse because it will cover the whole world. The way the world's economy looks now, the whole system could crash any day. But according to the Word of God, the economic system will rise even stronger than before, and when it is rebuilt, it will have a lot more control over the people to rule their lives. Verse 3 says, "His deadly wound was healed." Meaning, the economy is going to go back to what was before and even better. The devil tempted Jesus with all the kingdoms of the world and their glory, but Jesus would not bite the bait because He knew that it was only temporary and the Father's glory was eternal. Look at what happens when the first economic beast's wound is healed, and the second beast gives much more authority to the world system of men:

He was granted power to give breath to the image of the beast, that the image of the beast should both speak and cause as many as would not worship the image of the beast to be killed. He causes all, both small and great, rich and poor, free and slave, to receive a mark on their right hand or on their foreheads, and that no one may buy or sell except one who has the mark or the name of the beast, or the number of his name.

Revelation 13:15–17, NKJV

I do not necessarily believe that the mark is something that is going to be seen by man, but that it is a mark on the heart that trusts the system of man to take care of them rather than trusting Jesus to provide their daily needs. Even as God has a mark for His people, so the enemy marks his by what they trust in. Who do you really trust to provide for you? This matters. On which kingdom have we built our life: God's or the world system, which is the enemy's domain? If God told you to quit your job or move with no way of knowing where you would get your money from, would you do that? This is how you can know what kingdom foundation you are standing on.

When the devil is cast out of heaven, he will be enraged at the people who are earthbound and not dwelling in the heavens: "Therefore rejoice, O heavens, and you who dwell in them. Woe to the inhabitants of the earth and the sea. For the devil has come down to you, having great wrath, because he knows that he has a short time" (Revelation 12:12, NKJV). This is why God has given us the wings of a great eagle to fly to Him for safety and strength in His realm and not by receiving strength from the earthly realm. I hear the Spirit shouting, "Come up here, to him who has ears to hear, let him hear what the Spirit is saying to the church." Why should we be rejoicing in heaven when the devil is attacking the earthbound people? This does not seem right for a Christian to do. What makes this right is not that we are rejoicing that the people are being persecuted, but that we have overcome the beast system, the mark, and the number. This makes us overcomers to sit in the throne with Jesus: "And I saw something like a sea of glass mingled with fire, and those who have the victory over the beast, over his image and over his mark and over the number of his name, standing on the sea of glass, having harps of God" (Revelation 15:2, NKJV).

These overcomers who have overcome the system of man, which is being controlled through demonic powers, has placed in the world's grasp a new financial system that was wounded and has been healed. This is not from man; it is a world demonic system. "And all the world marveled and followed the beast" (Revelation 13:3, NKJV). But we who have overcome the system are following the Lamb of God wherever He goes. We are like the sea of glass in our spirit, for the peace of God will rule in our heart and God will crush Satan under our feet through His peace within.

To Christians, the numbers 666 are probably the most familiar numbers in the whole Bible. So much has been taught on 666 that worldly people speak of it also; people think that the mark is a computer chip under the skin. Many teach that this mark is *literally* in the forehead or hand. But as I see it, since six is the number of man, and man was created on the sixth day, 666 is the maturity or completeness of sin in fallen man (there are three sixes, and the number three means completeness). The seed of sin that was sown into man has completely matured in the people of the earth into the likeness of Satan. To be marked in the hand or forehead speaks prophetically about people's minds and how they think, and their hands act out only the ways of the world with God far from their thoughts.

We must ask God to free us up from trusting the world system to provide for our daily needs but to trust Him alone so that we can deliver the people who are calling out to God to save them. We are called to be God's deliverers even as Moses and Aaron delivered the people of Israel from Egypt with the glory that he received at the burning bush. Moses did not do it in his power but through the glory that was upon him. We must remember that the book of Revelation is a book of symbols and types. In fact, the first verse in chapter one declares this to be: "The Revelation of Jesus Christ, which God gave unto him, to show unto his servants things which must shortly come to pass; and he sent and signified it by his angel unto his servant John" (Revelation 1:1, KJV). The word *signified* means, "to make known through a sign or symbol." Most, if not all, of the book of Revelation is a book of symbols that we must seek for understanding.

God's Glory Manifested

> Arise, shine; For your light has come. And the glory of the Lord is risen upon you. For behold, the darkness shall cover the earth, and deep darkness the people; but the Lord will arise over you, and His glory will be seen upon you. The Gentiles shall come to your light, and kings to the brightness of your rising.
>
> Isaiah 60:1–3 (NKJV)

There is going to be a generation alive on earth that will receive the outpouring of His glory that He has promised in these verses. I believe *we* are that people. When Jesus came to earth, people could not believe that they could be the generation of the long-awaited Messiah. If now is not the time of His glory, when? Does not darkness cover the earth, and deep darkness the people? Then we can expect it. When you cannot turn on the TV for five minutes without hearing of perversion over and over, we're in darkness. When children are killing children for fun, we're in deep darkness. When churches are ordaining homosexuals, we're in deep darkness. We should not only believe that His glory is coming in a much greater way, but we must be expecting and

Dan Luehrs

preparing for it. Jesus said that the Scriptures must be fulfilled, and this is one of those.

Notice that Isaiah says, "His glory will be upon you." This excites me. If you have ever sensed the presence of God on you just once, you're hooked. I remember the first time I felt His presence. I was teaching my first Bible study, and after I was done teaching, I sat down, and it felt like I was glowing—like light was shining from me—for it was all so new to me. Then the next time I shared a testimony in a church service and it happened again. You might say that was just the anointing. Yes, but it was so real!

Just What Is the Glory?

We are to arise and shine when we sense His presence, because God's glory is manifested through our expressions of love to mankind. This means to do whatever He has laid on your heart to do at that time. There are many times I sense His presence, and it's not just when I'm preaching. It's been at the ball game when my sons were playing, at the bank, the beach, or up thirty-five thousand feet in an airplane. I would love to live in His presence twenty-four hours a day if I could. But I have found that when He comes, I have a job to do. It might be to pray, witness, write, or to just sit and wait on Him. It could be God confirming to me that this is His will for me to do something. In fact, it is very easy to get addicted to His presence and to rely on it all of the time. This has happened to me for a while until the Lord corrected me by showing me some Scripture on this: "But My righteous one shall live by faith..." (Hebrews 10:38). If we are walking by faith, we do not have to fear the system of the beast.

To live by faith is to fight the good fight of faith. But when we are in His presence, it does not take much faith whatsoever, for He is right there. God will give us times of refreshing that may go on for a few days like a spiritual vacation. This has given me much strength for the battle that is just ahead. A lot of people have learned to sit in His presence in this last out-pouring of His Spirit. Many come to services and just have soaked away in His presence for hours upon hours, for what? We are to be changed from glory to glory in His presence in order to be prepared for the battles that lay ahead. Most of the time, I need His presence daily, and He graciously gives His Spirit without measure. Think of it as rain that causes growth to come to the crops. What if it rained all the time? The crops would die for lack of sunshine. So it is in the spirit: we must have rain *and* sunshine to grow. Spiritual sunshine causes heat and stress to come in our lives. But I can thank God that He knows when I need rain or sun.

In Luke 3:21–22, Jesus was being water baptized and Holy Spirit baptized at the same time. He was being anointed for the ministry to which the Father had called Him. Did He go right into ministry when the anointing came? No, He went straight into the wilderness. That's great stress. In fact, when He was full of the Holy Spirit, the Spirit led Him there. We would never go there on our own if God were not going before us. When you are so hungry for God, you would follow Him anywhere or you would rather die because His presence means more to you than anything on this planet.

It's only after we are tested in the wilderness or under great stress that our obedience is really tested. Then we can be ready for ministry that God has prepared for us. This is why every person used of God must go through the wilderness experience. All the great saints have gone through it like Joseph, Moses, David, John the Baptist, Paul, and yes, even Jesus. If we would enter our ministry without going through the wilderness experience, God would have to apologize to these men. For it says of Jesus:

> And when the devil had finished every temptation [testing], he departed from Him until an opportune time. And Jesus returned to Galilee in the power of the Spirit; and news about Him spread through all the surrounding district.
>
> Luke 4:13–14 (NASB)

Dan Luehrs

It's only when self is broken that God can entrust us with great signs and wonders in ministry. If we are not broken of self, then the devil will have a heyday with us. Pride will eat us up from the inside out, and ministry will be over. God has prepared for Himself a group of people that have paid the price in the wilderness and have died to self, unlike the children of Israel that fought against God in rebellion for forty years when they were in the wilderness.

It is time for the church to arise and walk in the glory that Jesus is walking in. The glory will manifest itself as in Isaiah 61:1–4:

> The Spirit of the Lord GOD is upon me, Because the LORD has anointed me To bring good news to the afflicted; He has sent me to bind up the brokenhearted, To proclaim liberty to captives, And freedom to prisoners; to proclaim the favorable year of the LORD, And the day of vengeance of our God; To comfort all who mourn, To grant those who mourn in Zion, Giving them a garland instead of ashes, The oil of gladness instead of mourning, The mantle of praise instead of a spirit of fainting. So they will be called oaks of righteousness, The planting of the LORD, that He may be glorified. Then they will rebuild the ancient ruins, They will raise up the former devastation's, And they will repair the ruined cities, The desolation's of many generations.

This truly is the good news of the kingdom. Though it may be darker now than ever, I am looking for the light to come—aren't you?

Seeing Jesus Face-to-Face

For it is the God who commanded light to shine out of darkness, who has shone in our hearts to give the light of the knowledge of the glory of God in the face of Jesus Christ.

2 Corinthians 4:6 (NKJV)

Today is a new day for those who are seeking God in the face of Jesus Christ, for there is an open heaven for us to receive all that God has available for us. It is a day of miracles, signs, and wonders. Yet the greatest wonder of all is seeing Jesus face-to-face. Nowhere in Scripture does it say to seek miracles; we are told to seek God's face: "This *is* Jacob, the generation of those who seek Him, who seek your face" (Psalms 24:6, NKJV). Despite this invitation, it is sad to say that many in the church do not know how to seek the glory of God in the face of Jesus, so they seek for signs and wonders that after a while does not satisfy the longing of the heart because only the presence of Jesus does. Some Christians want to be changed into the likeness of Jesus, yet this will only come about from the inside out; it takes place when we behold the glory of God in the face of Jesus Christ. He is the glory of God, and He is calling us to behold Him as never before so that we are changed into His likeness in the process. Seeing Him is to have our spiritual eyes opened to beholding Him as truth and light, which gives us life and joy. How could we not be changed if we have really seen the Lord of glory?

A Movement of Life

The thief does not come except to steal and to kill and to destroy. I alone came in order that they might be possessing life, and that they might be possessing it in superabundance.

John 10:6 (Wuest Translation)

Superabundant life—who would not want it? We live in a culture of sin, sickness, and death. Sin is death; people love darkness rather than light. They would rather seek out the things of darkness before seeking the face of God. Why is this? Because they are ignorant of the knowledge of Jesus Christ. His truth will set our minds free to understand spiritual realities of how life is to be lived and how it operates around us in our daily life. People do not understand that when we walk in willful sin, we are opening the door for the enemy to come in our lives to steal, kill, and destroy what we have been rightfully given by God. For example, when we give in to unforgiveness, bitterness and anger are the result, and the enemy steals God's joy and peace from us. Likewise, when we give into greed then the love of money comes in rather than joy, peace, and true contentment with what

Dan Luehrs

we have been given and trusting God with our financial future. It all boils down to knowing and obeying the knowledge that we have been given in the Word of God. This is what the Bible says of the unbeliever: "Having their understanding darkened, being alienated from the life of God, because of the ignorance that is in them, because of the blindness of their heart" (Ephesians 4:18–19, NKJV). But with the believer this is not so because we have the knowledge of God's Word.

We live in a society that wants instant gratification rather than waiting for God to bring His will and purposes to pass in our lives. Yes, our flesh is impatient, but if we will wait upon the Lord for His timing and strength, He will not only give us what we need but also what we desire. Jesus came to give us His supernatural life every day so that we might live in peace and joy, but we must go after it. If we lived a greedy life, we would have to put forth the energy to make money, and when we are embittered with someone, we have to think negative thoughts of this person taking up valuable time and energy. Either way, we can live by faith or in the power of the flesh, but if we live the life of faith or being self absorbed we are going to have to put forth the energy to maintain our walk.

The more we seek the face of God with all our heart, the more we receive His presence for our time well-spent with Him: "But you, when you pray, go into your room, and when you have shut your door, pray to your Father who *is* in the secret *place; and* your Father who sees in secret will reward you openly" (Matthew 6:6–7, NKJV). When we walk out of our homes with a smile on our face and joy in our heart, it is because we have met with the King—we are being rewarded openly. But if we as Christians are always stressed out and over-burdened, we are not carring the burden of the Lord, which is light.

In my spirit, I feel and see a new wave of life breaking forth upon the earth that will change Christianity into something that is living and very vibrant. Soon every Christian that calls on the name of Jesus is going to experience His life and power to live their lives in the victory of His life. Right now, if most Christians would be honest, they would tell you that their faith and hunger for God is not what they would like it to be. We live in a culture of death because so many people are focused on all that is wrong with society and their own life rather than looking at God's abundant life that He has put right before their eyes, but most will not take the time to seek it.

We know that the gospel of Jesus Christ is the Word of life, but how many of us are experiencing His superabundant life on a daily basis? To do this, we must stop the enemy from throwing the cares of the world upon us and stealing the joy of receiving the life that Jesus died to give us. Part of the problem is that we do not know how to receive and maintain His daily life to walk in the superabundant lifestyle. By the time you finish reading this, you will not only know how to receive His daily life, but you will know how to give it away so that others will walk in it also—because His life is addicting.

Some twenty years ago, I was praying with someone else about a name for his ministry, and the Lord gave me the name Eternal Life Ministries. When I spoke the name out, the Lord said, "That is the name of your ministry." I did not know that I even had a ministry. So I just kept it in my heart and pondered on the name, thinking that it must be an evangelistic type ministry with that type of name, without realizing that the key word in the name is *life*. I just thought of it as a soul-winning ministry and not a ministry of life. Then He gave me Titus 1:2 as the motto verse for the ministry: "In the hope of eternal life, which God, who cannot lie, promised long ages ago." For years, I wondered about this verse because how could we hope for eternal life if we already had eternal life when we received Jesus in our hearts? I then knew that there was more to the ministry than just soul-winning. This ministry is about knowing, receiving, and experiencing the abundant life of God.

Dan Luehrs

Words of this Life

> Go, stand in the temple and speak to the people all the
> words of this life.
>
> Acts 5:20 (NKJV)

Peter was placed in prison by the high priest because he was
preaching the Word of God with power, and the religious system
did not like it and was jealous because people were turning to the
Lord in the thousands, in turn, taking people away from them.
The religious system threw Peter in jail for preaching life, but one
night, an angel came to Peter and opened the prison door and
told Peter to get back out there and preach the words of this life.
Peter was not to listen to all the religious arguments of his day;
he was to give the life of Jesus away to all that would listen and
receive God's power of life.

On the day of Pentecost, Peter and the others with him were
filled with the Holy Spirit; yet the Bible says that they were all
filled *again* with the Spirit in Acts 4:31, "And they were all filled
with the Holy Spirit, and they spoke the word of God with bold-
ness." The question remains, why did the people need to be filled
with the Holy Spirit again when it was only a few days since
Pentecost? Because we leak! God has made it so that we need
to be filled with the Holy Spirit every day, hour, and second if
we desire it. The Holy Spirit is the life of who we are; we must
stay connected to the source of our life. But the problem with
most Christians is that they do not stay filled with the Spirit of
God every day and then wonder why they are not enjoying the
abundant life of Jesus. God has made away for us to receive His
life each day, but we must seek for it and wait upon the Lord. If
we are lazy and will not seek after God with all our heart, we will
dry up on the vine; but if we will take the time to stay filled with
God, we will have His abundant life flowing through us daily.

> Then they entered into a covenant to seek the Lord
> God of their fathers with all their heart and with all
> their soul... And all Judah rejoiced at the oath, for they
> had sworn with all their heart and sought Him with all
> their soul; and He was found by them, and the Lord
> gave them rest all around.
>
> 2 Chronicles 15:12, 15 (NKJV)

Judah entered into a covenant with the Lord to seek Him with all their hearts, have you? Listen to the benefits they received; God was found by them, and they had rest. Few Christians today have true peace and rest within because of all the turmoil going on in the earth and in their own lives. God promises us rest if we will seek Him diligently with our whole being. God created man to fill with Himself; He wants humans to walk with Him in the cool of the day as Adam did. But Adam fell out of fellowship with God, and nothing is ever said that he walked with God again after this. I presume that he did. It was not until the life of Enoch that the Bible says a man walked with God, and God took him to Himself because he sought God diligently and knew that God would reward those who seek Him through faith. His faith of seeking God was rewarded with His likeness, and so will ours be if we seek Him with all of our heart in faith. Then He will reward us with His presence: "But without faith it is impossible to please Him, for he who comes to God must believe that He is, and that He is a rewarder of those who diligently seek Him" (Hebrews 11:6, NKJV). The Bible calls those *wise* who seek God, but to those who do not, they are foolish. I do not want to be one of the foolish virgins who misses his destiny because he would not take the time to seek after the face of God and keep his flasks filled. This is why we are to know what the will of God is and redeem the time that He has given to us and not to waste it.

Dan Luehrs

> Look carefully then how you walk. Live purposefully *and* worthily *and* accurately, not as the unwise *and* witless, but as wise [sensible, intelligent people], making the very most of the time [buying up each opportunity], because the days are evil. Therefore do not be vague *and* thoughtless *and* foolish, but understanding *and* firmly grasping what the will of the Lord is. And do not get drunk with wine, for that is debauchery; but ever be filled *and* stimulated with the [Holy] Spirit.
>
> Ephesians 5:15–18 (AMP)

These verses clearly tell us what the will of God is to ever be filled with the Holy Spirit. He is our comforter, friend, and the one who lives in us and walks beside us at all times. I have done a lot of traveling by myself to developing countries preaching the gospel, and I cannot think of one time that I did not feel the Holy Spirit's presence both in and upon me. He is ever-faithful to fill us if we will just ask Him. It is not only on the mission field that I sense His presence, but every day I have learned to practice the presence of the Lord. This is not just for a few chosen people; it is for all Christians to learn and cultivate. When we are staying filled every day with the Spirit of the Lord and are so in love with Jesus and are singing and thanking Him for all that He is allowing in our lives, both good and bad, His presence and glory in our lives will only grow. By doing this, we are constantly staying filled with God and are bringing glory to His name. I was once passing blood, and fear tried to come on me and I began to worship the Lord and said to Him, "Whether I live or die I am going to worship you!" That night while I was sleeping Jesus walked through my bedroom door and said, "Be healed." The next day the doctor could not find anything wrong with me!

> But be constantly controlled by the Spirit, speaking to one another in psalms and hymns and spiritual songs,

singing and making melody in your hearts to the Lord, giving thanks always concerning all things in the Name of our Lord Jesus Christ to God, even the Father, putting yourselves in subjection to one another in the fear of Christ.

Ephesians 5:19–21, (Wuest Translation)

We are redeeming our time when we do these things and seeking after the face of God; we each have been given only so much time, and God considers us wise if we are staying filled with His Spirit. We were not meant to live life without Him from the beginning of creation, and that is why we are to ever stay filled with the life of God. Adam and Eve were to eat daily from the Tree of Life, for that is what the Holy Spirit is: *life*. They had to take the time to pick and eat from the tree, and so must we. The way to the Tree of Life has been opened to us through Jesus Christ, and God expects us to eat from Him every day and all day if we desire to gain eternal life with Christ: "Do not labor for the food which perishes, but for the food which endures to everlasting life, which the Son of Man will give you, because God the Father has set His seal on Him" (John 6:27, NKJV). What I believe Jesus is saying is this: "Make it your life's work to seek after and eat of me and I will give you my eternal life." Eternal life is not time that goes on and on, it is Jesus Himself, and He desires to share His life with us. (See John 17:3.)

The Scriptures are very clear that all living things and all created things come from Jesus; all these things exist through His life and the power of His Word. We are called to be His bride, joint-heirs with Him, but we must understand what a bride is. It's a person that is equal to the other. You would not marry a dog or any other animal because it is not your counterpart, and neither did Adam: "So Adam gave names to all cattle, to the birds of the air, and to every beast of the field. But for Adam there was not found a helper comparable to him" (Genesis 2:20, NKJV). Jesus is looking for a suitable companion with all the right quali-

Dan Luehrs

ties (His character) to be His bride for all eternity and to share in ruling the kingdom of God on the earth. Just as Adam was called to rule with his wife, so we are called to rule with Jesus; He is our husband who already rules the universe and more.

Think of it this way. Jesus sits in His throne with all power and authority, the very life and presence of God flows from His person to all of creation. Around His one throne, there are many other thrones built where the saints of God will judge the angels and all nations. "And I saw thrones, and they sat on them, and judgment was committed to them…" (Revelation 20:4, NKJV). As an overcoming believer, Jesus is offering us a seat with Him to rule as His bride, and as great as that is, He is offering us to share His power and authority with Him. This power and authority is His very life and anointing that flows through Him from the throne, and He wants to share this with you. If you enjoy the trickle of God's presence flowing in and through your body now, just wait until you are on the throne with Him and His eternal life is flowing through you to give away to all creation throughout the universe. Now that is being swallowed up into life. Wow!

We now have a portion of God's life flowing in and through us as the angel witness to this truth when he commanded Peter to speak the words of life to all the people that were in the temple. He was to give away the life of Jesus to all that would receive from him. God's Spirit gives us life within because He is now living and abiding in us, He is the life-giving spirit: "And so it is written, "The first man Adam became a living being." The last Adam became a life-giving spirit" (1 Corinthians 15:45, NKJV). The first Adam received life from God and became a living being, but Jesus came giving life to all that would receive, and this is what we are to be doing with the life that we now have received. *We are to be life-giving beings.* We are to point people to Christ, to eat and drink of Him like we would partake of natural food and drink. We have the bread and water of life within us and must give it to all that want to partake of Him. Our words and actions can give life to another person as we go throughout our day.

The Ascending Lifestyle

Manifesting His Life

For we who live are always delivered to death for Jesus'
sake, that the life of Jesus also may be manifested in our
mortal flesh.

2 Corinthians 4:11 (NKJV)

There is one thing that all humans hate: suffering. Notice what
Paul is saying here: we who are alive must go through the dying
daily process for Jesus' sake so that His life might be manifested
through us. There is no other way for us to become the overcomers that God has called us to be other than the way of carrying
our daily cross to death. Nature teaches us this with the seeds
that have to die so that they may live again. We all get excited
about receiving and giving the anointing of Jesus away, but we do
not like or fully understand the dying process so that His life can
be manifested through us. It is this easy: no death, no life. You
might be wondering, "What is the dying process that we all must
go through?" Paul tells us:

We are hard-pressed [in tribulation] on every side,
yet not crushed; we are perplexed , but not in despair;
persecuted, but not forsaken; struck down [by people's
words], but not destroyed—always carrying about in
the body the dying of the Lord Jesus, that the life of
Jesus also may be manifested in our body.

2 Corinthians 4:8–10 (NKJV)

We are *always* carrying about this body of death with us. If we do
not take a bath, we stink, then we put on deodorant and perfume
to cover up the stench; and when we use the restroom, we have
to spray when we have finished. Why? Because death stinks to
the high heavens. Whether we are followers of Christ or not, we

Dan Luehrs

carry about this body of death around with us. But we who are believers carry even more death than the average person does because of the dying of Jesus. Our flesh is a clay pot that God has chosen to fill with the treasure of His glory, and because of this, the enemy of our souls wants to turn us away from serving the living God. He attacks our mind in every way possible to discourage us so that we feel crushed, despaired, forsaken, and destroyed. It's only an emotional feeling that makes it feel real to our mind, for it is based in fear of the unknown.

I had a dream one night wherein Jesus and I were standing outside of a carnival trailer, and we walked inside to see the freak show, and there was a puppet on the wall that had strings for its movement, and I said, "What is it?"

He said, "Satan." Fear arose in my heart, and as it did, the puppet came to life, and I ran out of the trailer, and the puppet was chasing me. When I awoke, I asked the Lord about it, and He said that Satan was like the Wizard of Oz, standing behind a curtain to see whom he could cause to walk in fear when he was only a small man with no real power.

God wants us to arise over the power of the enemy like fear, which means: False Evidence Appearing Real. It is up to us to fight, for God has given us the weapons of warfare, and we must seize the moment and become the warriors of God.

Going into the Depths of God

For to us God revealed them [the hidden mysteries] through the Spirit; for the Spirit searches all things, even the depths of God.

1 Corinthians 2:10 (NAS)

Endeavoring to write about God is a towering task, let alone writing about the depths of God. But the Scriptures beckon us to know His heart as intimately as lovers do. This is the depth of God that I am writing about, to know His heart as King David did and more. He was a man after God's own heart, and I desire to be one of those also. The Father is inviting us to know His heart and to search Him out, all the hidden treasures that He has for us are in our grasp if we will just take the time to be with Him on a daily basis and seek Him out. The desire of my heart is to know the intimate secrets of God; they are concealed in His heart, and

He wants to reveal them to all who will take the time to search for Him. There are no barriers to the Spirit of God for He searches out the depths of God; He also searches our heart and knows what is there. On top of all that, He wants to give us unlimited vision to see as far as He enables us to see into His heart.

I once had a mountaintop prophetic experience where there were no clouds, and I could look in any direction and see endlessly without any hindrance of the flesh whatsoever. I was totally free to see and experience the wonders of God. This has helped me to understand that God has given us an open heaven so that we might see what He has for us at this remarkable time in history. Present-day truth and the revelation of Jesus Christ is coming forth with such clarity now because the time is at hand for Jesus to manifest Himself through us. Unless we are prepared for it through the Word of God and the power of the Holy Spirit, we will miss what He has for us.

Most people love a good mystery, whether it is a book or movie so that they can figure out the hidden plot before they get to the end. Some like flea markets or seeking a lost treasure chest; when I was a child, I would love to explore the attic, barn, or a large closet of our home to see if I could find some lost treasure. I guess I have not changed too much because I still love searching for the unfathomable treasures in the depths of God's heart (His Word) to see the hidden mysteries in the ancient of days. All His treasures are waiting for us to find like the hidden gold in the mountains of California.

This was the desire of Moses when he asked God to show him His glory. Moses was intrigued with God when he saw Him in the burning bush, and then on the mountain he saw God's backside. He passed by, and Moses saw where God had been and where He was going. I believe all that Moses saw he wrote down in the book of Genesis because that is where God was—His history. God revealed the secrets of His heart to Moses, His friend, because he sought to know Him each day in the tent of meetings:

Dan Luehrs

"The secret [of the sweet, satisfying companionship] of the Lord have they who fear [revere and worship] Him, and He will show them His covenant *and* reveal to them its [deep, inner] meaning" (Psalms 25:14, AMP).

God will reveal the depths of His heart if we just ask Him, for He is no respecter of persons. God has revealed some of His past and future in the Word, but He wants us to receive the fullness of His Spirit, and His Spirit searches all the depths of God; this He has promised to give us in the book of Ephesians. When we seek and ask for His fullness, we must believe that it is His will for us and expect to receive it. Now that is faith. When we received our salvation and the baptism of the Holy Spirit (the down payment), it was because we asked God for it; and so will come the fullness of God to us, if we ask Him. In the year 1900, Charles Parham and a few young people sought God for the baptism of the Holy Spirit with the evidence of speaking in other tongues. They received Him because they asked outside the box of the mundane religious experience of the day. We also will receive all that God has for us in this day if we will just seek Him for the fullness of the spirit that He has promised in His Word.

> That [Spirit] is the guarantee of our inheritance [the firstfruits, the pledge and foretaste, the down payment on our heritage], in anticipation of its full redemption *and* our acquiring [complete] possession of it—to the praise of His glory.
>
> Ephesians 1:14 (AMP)

This is our purpose while we are living on earth: to receive His fullness. This is what Christianity is all about—the full life of Jesus flowing through us to give us vision, hope, and a purpose for living. We are to know and seek the depths of God and what are His width, length, depth, and height. (See Ephesians 3:18.) When we seek and walk in all of Him, we will be His bride, not having spot nor wrinkle or any such thing in us, having power and authority in Christ to do the greater works with Him. God wants to reveal His heart to us if we will just ask Him. Nobody will be able to probe the depths of who we are if we are hidden in God's heart, for only the Spirit of God is able to reveal such truth and glory to the children of men. " … But the spiritual man investigates indeed all things, but he himself is not being probed by anyone. For who has come to know experientially the Lord's mind, He who will instruct him? But as for us, Christ's mind we have" (1 Corinthians 2:12–14, Wuest translation).

Hear the Deep Calling You

> Deep calls unto deep at the noise of your waterfalls; all your waves and billows have gone over me
>
> Psalms 42:7 (NKJV)

If you have an unquenchable desire for God and pant after Him like the deer pants for the water, you are able to understand the depths of what God is calling you to in this relationship with Him. The way we thirst for God is to start seeking Him with all our heart and to taste and see that He is good. And once you have a taste for Him, you will thirst for more and more until you are seeking and searching for Him with your whole heart throughout the day. We must learn how to practice the presence of the Lord out of every minute of every day; our deep thirst for Him will require it, as an addict needs a fix. Jesus said that when we drink of His living waters, we would thirst no more. Meaning that nothing else in this world can satisfy the thirst of our spirit man once we have partaken of His life within.

The more we drink of Him each day, the more we want to drink until we are drinking from a waterfall of God's Spirit, which is giving us life from the throne. Think about it for a moment:

Dan Luehrs

what comes in us must go out. Jesus said in John 7:38, "He who believes in me, as the Scripture has said, out of his heart will flow rivers of living water." If rivers of living water are flowing from us to give life to others, then rivers of life have to be flowing *into* us, and this only comes about if we are drinking of Him. We must know how to get to the water of life each day for ourselves so that others can drink of His life, which comes from our inner most being. His life and presence will then flow through our words as we give forth God's glory and point them to the source of life—Jesus.

The depths of God are heard and seen by others in our spirit man as we allow Him to flow through us by His Spirit and calling us to go deeper in Him. As we start a lifestyle of seeking God every day, it may only be a trickle of His Spirit that we are receiving, but if we are faithful to seek Him diligently, it will become a waterfall that will feed the longing of our soul. Oh, the wonder of it when the waves of God's Spirit come upon us to satisfy our thirst for Him.

From the very depth of our heart, we are calling out to depths of God's to have a closer relationship with Him and others of like faith. This is the fellowship of the heart that God wants to give all His people, but many do not know how to seek the heart of God because they think that they are asking for too much, or that they might be disappointed because they did not receive it the way they thought they should. This is not God's problem; it's ours. He desires to give us all of Himself. We have as much of God as we want, but if we will ask Him to give us a greater capacity to receive more, we will get it. Even though we may have to suffer for a short season, the time will come when God will give us all of Himself if only we will cry out for more of Him.

A Lover's Heart

As two people fall in love, they open their hearts to one other like a flower in full bloom; they desire to know each other's heart intimately, to know their past and dreams for the future. Sharing their past makes them vulnerable to hurting each other in an argument, or maybe it is shared with another person whom they should not have in confidence. Knowing the truth in its entirety can hurt a relationship, but not sharing it could destroy it if it came out later. God knows all about us, and He still chooses to love us. If lovers are truly honest with each other and their hearts are open to be explored, they can look over the past and move on into their hopes and aspirations of life together tomorrow. This is how love should be because everyone has a past, even God. When lovers seek to know each other's heart, they become transparent, hiding nothing, and this is how God is with us. How do I know this? Because He made us like Himself, and He wants us to explore His heart as a lover. He invites us to come in, even though we may break His heart at times.

When people get married, they search each other out physically and how they may please one another, and really, that is what we are saying to God in spirit, "Search me out," which is even more intimate than sex could ever be because the heart is who we are. This is true transparency.

> Search me, O God, and know my heart: try me, and know my thoughts.
>
> Psalms 139:23 (KJV)

This is a great pleasure for those who are lovesick for the Lord because they want to be pure and holy for Him. Our heart is either a brick wall or it's a door that Jesus is knocking on to come in. God has opened His heart to us even as we have asked Him to enter ours. The heart can also be a home for someone we love

Dan Luehrs

or a prison for our own feelings that have been hurt in the past, and those feelings could be killing us if we do not go to God and get healed of our past hurts.

The heart of God is bigger than the universe itself; does He not fill the heavens and the earth? Even though we cannot begin to comprehend the vastness of God's creation in the natural, yet God bids us to come and seek out His heart: "Then I will give them a heart to know me, that I am the Lord; and they shall be my people, and I will be their God, for they shall return to me with their whole heart" (Jeremiah 24:7, NKJV). God desires us to know Him so much so that He gives us a heart (capacity) in our spirit to seek and understand Him. God is inviting us to go deep inside His heart to search Him out like a well that echoes back its depth; the mind cannot even begin to fathom His depths, but our heart can because we have His Spirit who searches all things out.

This is so wonderful because we can never be bored with God if we are really seeking Him. It's not possible to be bored with Him because He is more lovely than all of His creation, and creation is not boring. It is a love affair with God that can never be fully quenched. It is when we look deep inside the heart of God that we can feel a part of Him more and more. When we see His glory and power at work in our lives, we are in awe, and we must come to understand that the more trials that we come through successfully, the greater our spirit is expanded to receive more of God. Science tells us that the universe is expanding and so is our heart if we are responding to our trials with thanksgiving and praise because these are the things that create the greatness of Jesus Christ in us.

> And the child grew and became strong in spirit, filled with wisdom; and the grace of God was upon Him.
>
> Luke 2:40 (NKJV)

If Jesus needed to grow strong in spirit, so must we. Do not fear your trials but embrace them to grow in spirit. True love never quits, and if we truly love God, we will not quit when we are under trial, but we will seek to draw even closer to Him in our heart. Many servicemen have gone to war with a special love for a girl in their heart, and some have told how that love kept them alive with hope of seeing them again someday. So must our love for Jesus keep us going to please Him in all respects because love never fails nor does it quit—ever.

Receiving the Spirit of Revelation

> God, our God, will take care of the hidden things but the revealed things are our business. It's up to us and our children to attend to all the terms in this Revelation.
>
> Deuteronomy 29:29 (The Message)

The revelation of God's truth is revealed to us when we seek the depths of His heart because that is where it is hidden, and He shares His secrets with those who continually draw close.

> It has been given to you to know the mysteries of the kingdom of heaven …
>
> Matthew 13:11 (NKJV)

All the treasures of wisdom and knowledge are hidden in the person of Jesus Christ; He is the key of knowledge. Carnally minded people seek natural understanding, but a spiritually minded person seeks spiritual wisdom from above that is beyond the mind of man. In fact, it is foolishness to him. True spiritual wisdom first seeks to know the person of Jesus Christ and follows Him in righteousness and truth. As we learn to obey His prompting, He will lead us into greater trials that will take more faith so that

Dan Luehrs

self-life in us has to die, and then Christ is raised above self so that He might live in and through us so that my mind, eyes, and hands are totally yielded to His Lordship and not my own.

We may gather many things to ourselves in this earthly life, but if we do not gain Christ, we are the biggest losers in the end. Paul said, "I have suffered the loss of all things, and count them as rubbish, that I may gain Christ…" (Philippians 3:8, NKJV). When we begin to see all our earthly possessions as garbage compared to the unfathomable riches of Christ and we choose to praise God in the midst of our trials, knowing that He is blessing us with them to know Him more. This takes a revelation from God to even think of praising Him in the face of trial because the natural man wants to murmur and complain. We are called to live a supernatural life that is beyond the world's way and much of the church's understanding. We are to live life out of the realm of the Spirit of God and not the natural mind or the realm of darkness, for we are sons of light.

When we begin to perceive that the full revelation of Jesus Christ is worth losing everything in this world, we can then begin to walk through our tribulations knowing that God desires to reveal more of His Son in us: "Again, the kingdom of heaven is like a merchant seeking beautiful pearls, who, when he had found one pearl of great price, went and sold all that he had and bought it" (Matthew 13:45, NKJV). The full revelation of Jesus does not come from studying books and receiving head knowledge—no, it comes by the Holy Spirit giving us one truth of revelation on top of another through our lifetime and seeing if we will be faithful to what He has given us. In fact, unless we get a fresh revelation of the Son of God, we will not make it through the greater trials of life because demonic powers will try to steal the seed that has been planted in our heart. But as we win the battle, ground will be taken in the realm of our soul, and we will be free to go on to receive the greater revelation of Jesus Christ until one day

He manifests Himself in and through us. Every nugget of truth given to us is a revelation of Jesus because Jesus is the truth.

The book of Revelation is called the Revelation of Jesus Christ; it is not the revelation of the end times. The book reveals Jesus in and through the body of Christ. It starts out with much of the church being caught up in worldliness, and she ends up in the last chapters as the bride of Christ having the glory of God on the throne. (See Revelation 21:11.) How was she changed into His glory? By going through great tribulation. "These are they which came out of great tribulation, and have washed their robes, and made them white in the blood of the Lamb" (Revelation 7:14, KJV). Please hear me in this: The book of Revelation is about the church coming through great tribulation to become the bride of Christ. All that is happening in the pages between the front and the back of the book is the outworking of what Jesus is doing in us (the church).

If you have given your life to Jesus, you are now living the pages of the book of Revelation through your lifetime and are being changed into the bride of Christ. I once told a friend that I felt we were already in the book of Revelation, and he looked at me like I had lost my mind; but I knew in my spirit I was right, and God showed me this truth some years later in the Bible. Jesus said in Revelation 1:1 that these things would "come to pass quickly" (YLT). I believe that the "quickly" came to pass when Jesus gave the message to John on the Isle of Patmos. The church of today wants to see the book of Revelation played out on the world's stage when God is having it played out *in* us. We just don't know it.

Do you know of any Christians that are truly seeking God and are not going through some kind of tribulation in their life? If our hearts' desire is to have Jesus manifested in and through us, then the only way for this to happen is to have the book of Revelation (tribulation) worked out in us. This is the only way for Him to come forth from us; the Lion of the tribe of Judah devours our flesh, for that is what lions do, eat flesh. No one enters into all that God has for them unless they come through the door of tribulation, and that is what the book of Revelation is a symbol of (Acts 14:22).

"Happy is he who is reading, and those hearing, the words of the prophecy, and keeping the things written in it—for the time is nigh" (Revelation 1:3, YLT). Most people are not happy to read or hear about the book of Revelation because they do not understand that it pertains to them receiving the full likeness of Jesus. If Christians would understand that Jesus is preparing them through their tribulations, they would be happy to go through it with Him: "Blessed [happy] is the man who perseveres under trial, because when he has stood the test, he will receive the crown of life [the likeness of Jesus] that God has promised to those who love him" (James 1:12, NIV). How many more promises do we need from God to finish our course with the joy and to receive the crown of life?

The First Seal Broken

> Now I saw when the Lamb opened one of the seals; and I heard one of the four living creatures saying with a voice like thunder, "Come and see." And I looked, and behold, a white horse. He who sat on it had a bow; and a crown was given to him, and he went out conquering and to conquer.
>
> Revelation 6:1–2 (NKJV)

Now look what happens when the first seal is broken on the book that only Jesus can open: the rider (Jesus) goes out to conquer us for He has already conquered sin and death. Each time one of the seals is opened on the book, new judgments are being released upon us to kill the man of sin in us. Jesus is riding this white horse to conquer you and me. Who do you think He is going out to conquer? It is our flesh. The life of Jesus Christ is hidden within us, and as we go through our tribulations, He is opening the seals so that our self-life may be killed; then the life of Jesus will come forth to bring His life to the world.

> For we who live are always delivered to death for Jesus' sake, that the life of Jesus also may be manifested in our mortal flesh.
>
> 2 Corinthians 4:11–12 (NKJV)

Notice what Paul is saying here: we all must go through the dying process so that the life of Jesus will be manifested through us. There is no other way for us to be overcomers than the way of death. Does not nature teach us this with the seeds that have to die so that they may live again?

When the seventh seal is broken and the seventh angel sounds forth, then the kingdoms of this world become the kingdoms of our Lord and His Christ. Our self-kingdom must be dead in us so that His kingdom might reign through us.

> Then the seventh angel sounded: And there were loud voices in heaven, saying, "The kingdoms of this world have become the kingdoms of our Lord and of His Christ, and He shall reign forever and ever."
>
> Revelation 11:15 (NKJV)

It is through great tribulation of this kind that we are conquered, and so must every Christian come through as an overcomer. This is why the King of kings comes in the book of Revelation to do warfare in us so that He may work through us to conquer the rest of mankind. When we are fully conquered, we get to help others in this dying process so that He might live His life through them also. "Now I saw heaven opened, and behold, a white horse. And

Dan Luehrs

He who sat on him was called Faithful and True, and in righteousness He judges and makes war. And the armies in heaven, clothed in fine linen, white and clean, followed Him on white horses" (Revelation 19:11, 14). As we overcome through our tribulations, which are the judgments of God in our life, then we are considered faithful to serve with Jesus to help the rest of mankind become overcomers also. Hallelujah.

Your Destiny

The Throne

Today, there is all kinds of talk about our hidden calling or destiny while we are on earth. Such books as *The Secret* and other new-age books like it declare that we are the masters of our lives, and if we just name and claim it, we can have it. But is such thinking true? To a point it is, but it can run amuck very quickly, leading us off the path of life that God has called us to, instead leading us to a ditch of our own creation, only bringing more pain and sorrow in the end. Every person who has ever lived has had a desire within to be someone important or to do something great or to plainly put it, to make a name for themselves. God has put this desire of greatness in us, but the flesh wants to do its own thing right now and does not want to wait for God's timing, so the carnal man will try anything to become important in the eye's of man without any suffering whatsoever if possible.

If I were to tell every Christian that God has invited them to the highest seat of authority in His creation, most would not or could not believe such a thing. When I talk with some Christians about this, they don't even know that Jesus has called them to sit with Him in His throne. Some people look at me like I fell off my rocker. Don't argue with me about it. Jesus said it, so why not believe it?

> To him that overcometh will I grant to sit with me in my throne, even as I also overcame, and am set down with my Father in his throne.
>
> Revelation 3:21, KJV

You can either believe the gospel or reject it (heresy), but you will only do it to your own great loss. Most people reading this believe Jesus when He said, "I am the way, and the truth, and the life; no one comes to the Father, but through me" (John 14:6, NAS). They believe Him because they know that they are sinners in need of a Savior, but that's all they can believe because they see how bad they are and cannot see the goodness of God to not only forgive them but exult them to a place of authority in His kingdom. Know this for sure that God's kingdom will rule over all one day whether they like it or not. And when His kingdom manifests, God is going to have people ready to rule and reign with Him that He is going to give authority to.

> And he said to him, "Well done, good slave, because you have been faithful in a very little thing, be in authority over ten cities."
>
> Luke 19:17–18 (NAS)

I do not believe that Jesus is speaking figuratively here. Jesus now rules and reigns and is soon coming back to take over what He has purchased with His blood to give to all His prepared ones.

Dan Luehrs

Then the sovereignty, the dominion, and the greatness of all the kingdoms under the whole heaven will be given to the people of the saints of the Highest One; His kingdom will be an everlasting kingdom, and all the dominions will serve and obey Him.

Daniel 7:27 (NAS)

Visions of Glory

I want to share two prophetic experiences with you that have helped me understand the throne of fire and our calling into it.

In 1996, I had a vision of a preacher being set on fire. I saw him preaching in a service, and he was like a walking matchstick with arms and legs. At first just his head was on fire, then suddenly, the whole matchstick was consumed with fire. I said to the Lord, "What was that all about?" He gave me Hebrews 1:7: "I am making my ministers a flame of fire." The Lord confirmed this vision to me through Rick Joyner's book *The Call.* In the book, he speaks about how the Lord showed him that these messengers of fire are about ready to be released in the church to bring repentance so that we will be prepared for His glory.

For over ten years now, the Lord has been pouring fresh oil of His Spirit on His church, and He is about to set it on fire to burn for Him. We will not have to announce this fire. People will just come to watch us burn. This will be the baptism of fire that we have been waiting for. Jesus promised us that we would be baptized with fire, and our Father is the fire that will now consume us. He will burn all the wood and hay out of our lives. Those who are purified will do the greater works of Jesus Christ.

Jesus was baptized with fire at His baptism, and His apostles were set on fire at Pentecost. Now it's our turn. Hallelujah! There is something coming even greater than what they had, I tell you, what I see coming is Isaiah 60:1: "Arise, shine: your light has come. And the glory of the Lord has risen upon you." I get excited about this because these are the greatest days to be alive. The words *arise upon you* means to "shoot forth as beams of light, as the sun." Only life can give forth life; death cannot bring forth life. When the lights are turned on, all darkness must flee. As we go forth with His glory, great healing and deliverance shall take place, and nothing shall be able to stand against Him. Now is the time when His glory is going to be revealed in the earth through His people to a dying world. "And nations will come to your light, and kings to the brightness of your rising" (Isaiah 60:3).

Jesus came to me as I was sitting on a dock by a lake on May 17, 2000; His presence came upon me. For about a week, I had not been able to get into His presence very well, but that night, He came powerfully. He came to me and said, "Do you want to go up higher?"

I thought, *There is more?*

He said, "Yes, my glory."

Then I said, "Yes, I want this."

He said, "Follow me."

After this, a messenger came with a container of water.

Then Jesus said, "Cup your hands."

As I did, the angel filled them up, and Jesus said, "Now wash your face and eyes and ears." Then the angel filled my hands again, and Jesus said, "Now drink."

I said, "What is this?"

He said, "My cup."

Then I knew what this was about.

> And He said to her, "What do you wish?" She said to Him, "Command that in your kingdom these two sons of mine may sit, one on your right and one on your left." But Jesus answered and said, "You do not know what you are asking for. Are you able to drink the cup that I am about to drink?" They said to Him, "We are able." "My cup you shall drink; but to sit on my right and on

Dan Luehrs

my left, this is not mine to give, but it is for those for whom it has been prepared by my Father."

Matthew 20:21–23

Jesus therefore said to Peter, "Put the sword into the sheath; the cup which the Father has given me, shall I not drink it?" (John 18:11). Many of us want to come into all that the Lord has for us, but are we willing to drink from His cup of suffering? "If we suffer, we shall also reign with him: if we deny him, he also will deny us" (2 Timothy 2:12).

Stanley Frodsham prophesied this word in 1965:

> Understand these two things and meditate upon them solemnly: the persecution and the darkness shall be as great as the glory, in order to try and turn the elect and the anointed ones from the path the Lord has laid down for them. Many shall start, but few shall be able to finish because of the greatness of grace that shall be needed to be able to endure unto the end. Understand that the way toward the glory is fraught with great danger, and many shall fall to the right and the left; many shall camp on lesser ground.

A Throne of Fire

Then I looked, and behold, a whirlwind was coming out of the north, a great cloud with raging fire engulfing itself; and brightness was all around it and radiating out of its midst like the color of amber, out of the midst of the fire. Also from within it came the likeness of four living creatures. And this was their appearance: they had the likeness of a man.

Ezekiel 1:4–5 (NKJV)

For years I have asked the Lord about Ezekiel's vision in chapter one and the experience that he had by the river Chebar. It all seemed so complicated to me, and I have never heard anyone give any explanation to the chapter that my spirit agreed with. I believe that the Lord has given me some insights into this wonderful chapter to help us understand the times that we have been called to live in.

Notice that the whirlwind was on fire, and within the fire, there were four living beings in the form of a human being. It's not that the cloud was anything, but that the cloud carried the glory of God within it. The cloud was a shroud of sorts like a spiritual body, or as our natural body is now a shroud of the glory of God in us. Hebrews 12:1 says, "We have so great a cloud of witnesses surrounding us." We, the church, the overcomers, are the cloud that the Lord of glory will appear in to all the nations of the earth. We have been invited into this great cloud of witnesses to manifest the Lord's glory: "Behold, He is coming with [or in] the clouds, and every eye will see Him, even those who pierced Him; and all the tribes of the earth will mourn over Him. Even so. Amen" (Revelation 1:7, NAS). (See also Mark 14:62 and Jude 14.) Why does Jesus have to come in the cloud? To reap the harvest of the earth.

> And I looked, and behold, a white cloud, and sitting on the cloud was one like a son of man, having a golden crown on His head, and a sharp sickle in His hand. And He who sat on the cloud swung His sickle over the earth; and the earth was reaped.
>
> Revelation 14:14, 16 (NAS)

An angel came to me in January 2007 and said, "One billion people are about to come into the kingdom. You must be ready." I believe it.

Dan Luehrs

We, the church, are the ministers of fire in the cloud that the Lord is coming in and through. How can anything live in fire? To put it simply: our God is a consuming fire, and we were created in His likeness, so that means that we were made to be creatures of fire also. Colossians 1:12 says, "Giving thanks to the Father, who has qualified us to share in the inheritance of the saints in light [in fire]." We are to be partakers of God's fire; this is our inheritance. You may protest and say that fire is for judgment. Please understand that hell's fire is hot because those there are not like God with their sin, and they are experiencing God as judgment, not as a blessing. But we who know God embrace His fire. I have experienced God's fire on many occasions, but once the fire was so hot that the person sitting next to me felt it, and we both began to just shout in glorious wonder at what we were experiencing. As Christians, His fire should be our desire.

God has other beings of fire: "And another angel, the one who has power over fire, came out from the altar" (Revelation 14:18, NAS). This angel was created to be in the fire of the altar to be a minister of fire. "And of the angels He says, 'Who makes His angels winds, and His ministers a flame of fire'" (Hebrews 1:7, NAS).

Back to Ezekiel's vision of the fiery living beings.

> In the midst of the living beings there was something that looked like burning coals of fire, like torches darting back and forth among the living beings. The fire was bright, and lightning was flashing from the fire.
>
> Ezekiel 1:13 (NAS)

The very core of their being was fire. Not that they were on fire, but that they were the fire in the cloud. The fire in them was bright, meaning to have extreme brightness or radiance as the sun. Did not Jesus say that we would shine forth as the sun? We are to arise and shine. These fiery, living beings are what I saw in my vision of the preacher being set on fire to preach the gospel in these last days. God wants to set us on fire because His throne is fire (Daniel 7:9, NAS). If we are called to sit *in* His throne, who is a consuming fire, then we too will be beings of fire.

> Now above the expanse that was over their heads there was something resembling a throne, like lapis lazuli [sapphire] in appearance; and on that which resembled a throne, high up, was a figure with the appearance of a man. Then I noticed from the appearance of His loins and upward something like glowing metal that looked like fire all around within it, and from the appearance of His loins and downward I saw something like fire; and there was a radiance around Him. As the appearance of the rainbow in the clouds on a rainy day, so was the appearance of the surrounding radiance. Such was the appearance of the likeness of the glory of the Lord. And when I saw it, I fell on my face and heard a voice speaking.
>
> Ezekiel 1:26–28 (NAS)

What Ezekiel saw in his vision was another realm or dimension in the earth, and it is a throne with a man of fire on it. Jesus sits on the Father's throne in fire just as He walked in the fire with Shadrach, Meshach, and Abednego with no harm done to Him. Within the earth, there are many different realms such as the fire world within the earth or the water world where all the creatures can live in their environment, and without it, they will die. Then there is the bug world that lives inside the earth, and there are the birds that live and soar in the skies above the earth. Then there is a world where man and other mammals live on the earth, and let us not forget the bacteria world. So we can see that there are many different earthly realms right around us. Well, my friend, so is the spirit world; there are different spiritual realms that God has created. "In the beginning God created the heavens and the earth" (Genesis 1:1, NAS). Notice the word *heavens* is plural, meaning more than one. The word *heaven* is just another term for the spiritual world around us that God, angels, and the redeemed saints dwell in. But also there is the dark heaven or spiritual world where the devil, demons, and the ungodly people dwell. Hell is not a physical place but rather a spiritual realm where they exist.

The Bible says that we see through a glass darkly, and I want to show you what I am seeing through my spiritual looking glass. As far as we know from Scripture, there are three realms in the spirit world (2 Corinthians 12:2). There could be seven realms in the spirit world as far as we know, but one thing is for certain, one realm is the highest: God's throne realm. This is where all the authority over His creation is, and He has given that authority to a man (Matthew 28:18). The Father, Jesus, and the overcoming saints dwell in the highest realm together throughout eternity: "To him that overcometh will I grant to sit with me in my throne, even as I also overcame, and am set down with my Father in his throne" (Revelation 3:21). This is why the Scripture says that we sit *in* the throne and not *on* the throne because it is a realm and not a stationary position in the sky or on some planet where people sit on an ivory throne. That is an earthly example of true spiritual authority. Sitting on an earthly throne is an example of what true spiritual authority is. While we are on earth, we sit in heavenly places with Him, but the highest of these spiritual places is the throne realm. You are called unto this realm.

What Ezekiel saw in the spirit was the throne realm manifesting before him, and the greatest thing about this is that a man was on the throne. I believe that the man was Jesus, and we are to be one in Him to bring His kingdom to earth to rule and reign with Him. "Thy kingdom [throne, authority] come, Thy will be done in earth as it is in heaven" (Matt 6:10, NASV). In the end, God's throne realm will dictate all that goes on in the earth throughout eternity. "Thy throne is established from of old; Thou art from everlasting" (Psalms 93:2, NAS).

Four Living Creatures

> And before the throne there was, as it were, a sea of glass
> like crystal; and in the center and around the throne,
> four living creatures full of eyes in front and behind.
>
> Revelation 4:6, NAS

The four living creatures in the books of Ezekiel and Revelation
are found around and in the middle of the throne; they dwell in
the throne of fire. The number *four* in Scripture means "to rule,
reign, to overcome." I believe that the four living creatures represent the overcoming sons of God because they sit in the center of
the throne where we are called to be. These four living creatures
are the carriers of the throne (glory) of God.

> And I looked, and behold, in the midst of the throne
> and of the four living creatures, and in the midst of the
> elders, stood a Lamb as though it had been slain, having
> seven horns and seven eyes, which are the seven Spirits
> of God sent out into all the earth.
>
> Revelation 5:6–7 (NKJV)

Did you notice where Jesus is standing? Right in the middle of
the throne and in the middle of the four living creatures and
elders because that is where He is right now—in us. Now read
very carefully the next verses, and you will see clearly that we are
the living creatures, or should I say, the beings that have been
swallowed up into God's life. (See 2 Corinthians 5:4.)

Now when He had taken the scroll, the four living creatures
and the twenty-four elders fell down before the Lamb, each having a harp and golden bowls full of incense, which are the prayers
of the saints.

Dan Luehrs

And they sang a new song, saying:
You are worthy to take the scroll,
And to open its seals;
For You were slain,
And have redeemed us to God by Your blood
Out of every tribe and tongue and people and nation,
And have made us kings and priests to our God;
And we shall reign on the earth.

Revelation 5:9–10 (NKJV)

It is most certain from these verses that the living beings and twenty-four elders are redeemed saints on the throne of God, for only the redeemed of God sing a new song, for no angel has ever been redeemed by the blood of the Lamb. These on the throne are the overcomers, the rulers of the earth.

I have heard of people going to heaven and seeing those who dwell in the throne, and they had no way of describing the glory of those who sat there. All that John the apostle knew was that they were full of the life of God. Both John and Ezekiel called them *living* creatures because they were obviously full of life, and they had no other way of describing them. Their symbolism is this: the throne is full of life, and that which has life moves like a river. The Holy Spirit moved and still moves on the earth, as does the throne of God because it has wheels and wheels represent movement: "His throne was ablaze with flames, its wheels were a burning fire" (Daniel 7:9, NAS). "To Him who rides upon the highest heavens [the throne], which are from ancient times..." (Psalms 68:33, NAS). God does not rule from a stationary throne but from one that moves with Him because His throne is His authority. God's throne moved wherever the living creatures moved because the authority moved with them, the throne was within them. "Now as I looked at the living beings, behold, there was one wheel on the earth beside the living beings, for each of the four of them" (Ezekiel 1:15, NAS). They are the carriers and movers of the throne or authority of God. They were in it, and it was within them.

And whenever the living beings moved, the wheels moved with them. And whenever the living beings rose from the earth, the wheels rose also. Wherever the spirit was about to go, they would go in that direction. And the wheels rose close beside them; for the spirit of the living beings was in the wheels. Whenever those went, these went; and whenever those stood still, these stood still. And whenever those rose from the earth, the wheels rose close beside them; for the spirit of the living beings was in the wheels.

Ezekiel 1:19–21 (NAS)

Ezekiel chapter one finishes with "Such was the appearance of the likeness of the glory of the LORD. And when I saw it, I fell on my face and heard a voice speaking" (Ezekiel 1:26–28, NAS). All things described in chapter one are the glory of God—the throne, the man, and the living creatures on fire, is the glory of God. The night that Jesus came to me on the lake, He told me that there was another level that He called "My glory." I believe that the throne realm is the glory level that I am trying to write about here for I have wondered about this level for years, and now I am getting some revelation on it. Jesus said:

And the glory which Thou hast given me I have given to them; that they may be one, just as we are one; I in them [the throne], and Thou in me, that they may be perfected in unity, that the world may know that Thou didst send me, and didst love them, even as Thou didst love me.

John 17:22–23

His glory will make us one with Him and each other in the throne.

There are four different faces, one on each of the living beings, which represent a lion, a calf or an ox, a man, and an eagle.

Dan Luehrs

And before the throne there was, as it were, a sea of glass like crystal; and in the center and around the throne, four living creatures full of eyes in front and behind. And the first creature was like a lion, and the second creature like a calf, and the third creature had a face like that of a man, and the fourth creature was like a flying eagle. And the four living creatures, each one of them having six wings, are full of eyes around and within...

Revelation 4:6–8 (NAS)

The four faces of the living beings are four characteristics of the overcoming sons of God; they are not some weird-looking, hideous creatures upon the throne scaring people as they pass by. No, these are four declarations of their power and authority with the Son of God on the throne. In them is manifested the attributes of the life of God who share the throne with Him. They represent the life and character of God; they are living beings full of life, power, grace, wisdom, and glory. Preston Eby wrote of these living beings in his series of articles called, "From the Candlestick to the Throne."

Ah, precious friend of mine, if you have received the call of the overcomer to sit with HIM in His throne, then all that the four Living Creatures represent is even now being wrought out in your life, their nature becomes your nature, for naught but the nature of the Lamb and of the four Living Creatures can stand in the midst of the throne.

The Cherubim

Then the cherubim rose up. They are the living beings that I saw by the river Chebar.

Ezekiel 10:15 (NAS)

Some would argue the case about us being the living beings because Ezekiel said plainly in verse 15 that they are cherubim. The cherubim only prove my point even more because there are many types and shadows in Scripture that point to their true identity in another person or thing. For instance, Joseph, Moses, David, and others are all types of Christ in the Old Testament. The tabernacle in the wilderness and the feasts of Israel are all Old Testament shadows that point to Jesus and to New Testament truths and experiences. Colossians 2:17 says, "Things which are a mere shadow of what is to come; but the substance belongs to Christ." The substances of all shadows are summed up in Christ, or in other words, they point to Him and are fulfilled in Him.

To understand the cherubim, we must go back to the law of first use or the first time that they are used in Scripture to help us understand their function. They are first found in Genesis 3:24 as protectors of the Tree of Life: "So He drove the man out; and at the east of the Garden of Eden He stationed the cherubim, and the flaming sword which turned every direction, to guard the way to the tree of life." Remember that life flows from the throne, and the Tree of Life is found at the throne in Revelation 22:2. So we can see that the cherubim from the beginning are found around the throne and are protectors, if you will, of the life of God. By that, I mean, they don't protect God, but from people getting to the life of God before they come through Jesus alone.

The next time we find them in Scripture is in Exodus 25:18: "And you shall make two cherubim of gold, make them of ham-mered work at the two ends of the mercy seat." Again, they are found covering or protecting—this time, the mercy seat of God, which represents the glory and the presence of God, His author-ity on earth. They are in and around His throne. In fact, they are woven into the fabric all around the tabernacle both inside and out: "Moreover you shall make the tabernacle with ten curtains of fine twisted linen and blue and purple and scarlet material; you shall make them with cherubim, the work of a skillful workman" (Exodus 26:1, NAS). The picture of the throne in the book of Revelation is one with living creatures or cherub in and around it, just as the tabernacle in the wilderness.

> Who serve a copy and shadow of the heavenly things, just as Moses was warned by God when he was about to erect the tabernacle; for, "See, He says, 'that you make all things according to the pattern which was shown you on the mountain.'"
>
> Hebrews 8:5 (NAS)

We, the body of Christ, the bride, the sons of God, are the true reality of what is both in and around the throne. We are the carriers of the presence and glory of God in the earth; the cherubim were the Old Testament shadow, and the body of Christ is the reality of the shadow in and around the throne.

> These are the living beings that I saw beneath the God of Israel by the river Chebar; so I knew that they were cherubim.
>
> Ezekiel 10:20 (NAS)

Notice how Ezekiel says that the living beings were under God, not just under the throne alone as he describes in Ezekiel 1:26, but that God rides upon the cherubim, for they are the carriers of God's glory. "And He rode upon a cherub and flew; and He sped upon the wings of the wind" (Psalms 18:10, NAS).

I have had two prophetic experiences with the cherub that has helped me to understand their reality. The times that I saw them, I was praying with others, and the glory of the Lord was manifest in the room. The cherubim were surrounding us in a full circle like they were in the Holy of Holies. Their wings were raised and touching each other, protecting us like we were precious jewels; like the Ark of the Covenant that stood in the Holy of Holies.

This is because we are more precious; His presence abides with us and is in us even as He was in the holiest place in the temple. During one of these experiences, I had one of the most powerful words I have ever spoken; the Holy Spirit spoke through me, saying, "You are carriers of my glory." If we could just get a glimpse of this, we would stop wallowing around in this earthen clay experience of life and start seeking the things that are above and are true reality and life.

To Ride the Lightning

> And the living beings ran to and fro like bolts of lightning.
>
> Ezekiel 1:14 (NAS)

Do you want to ride the lightning? You will. This is what the living beings do; they are translated from one place to another by the will of God. Remember when Jesus walked through walls, walked on water, and brought the boat to land immediately in the midst of the storm, or when Philip was taken up from the eunuch?

> And when they came up out of the water, the Spirit of the Lord snatched Philip away; and the eunuch saw him no more, but went on his way rejoicing. But Philip found himself at Azotus; and as he passed through he kept preaching the gospel to all the cities, until he came to Caesarea.
>
> Acts 8:39–40 (NAS)

There will be no need for airline tickets or waiting at airports, for God's Lightning Line will be on time all the time. I believe that we will move even faster than the speed of light to the speed of God's thought, which will catch us up to His throne.

Dan Luehrs

The Twenty-Four Elders

For months, the Lord has been speaking to me about the number *twenty-four*; everywhere I seemed to look I saw *twenty-four*. For many months before this, the Lord was speaking to me about the number *four* until one day, it cumulated at Moravian Falls, North Carolina. That day, I went up in the mountains, and as I was coming down, I saw a mailbox that was number *forty-four*. I then looked at my phone, and the time said 4:44 p.m. I then looked at the miles per tank full, and it said 444. Then what happened was really weird—my temperature gauge on my car said forty-four when it was eighty outside. I bought a mirror that day, which was forty-four dollars, and I was forty-four years old when this all happened. The number *four* stands for sonship in its highest order; it means to rule and reign with Jesus. God is giving me the grace to stand and not fall, to overcome, to rule and reign in my personal life and the life to come.

A few months later, I was on my way home, and the Lord spoke to me and said, "Your new number is twenty-four that you will now be seeing." And sure enough, I began to see twenty-four everywhere. So I thought, *Well, this is just the power of suggestion, or like when you buy a car, and you never really noticed that kind of car before on the road until you bought one, then they are everywhere.* So I devised a plan; I will change the number to thirty-five and see how many times a day I would see it. Do you know how many times I saw thirty-five? None. So I began to seek the Lord about what twenty-four means for me. The number *two* is a number meaning "union," and *four* is "sonship"; so it must mean "the union of the overcomers." I did meet other Christians in the country that knew about the sons of God message, but I was still looking for more until I read Preston Eby's revelation on the twenty-four priests in the books of 1 Chronicles and Revelation, and then I had a fuller understanding of what God was saying to me.

Preston writes:

This great truth reveals why God placed the camp of the priests directly *between* Himself and the people of Israel. It should be clear to any thinking mind that the priesthood camped "round about" the tabernacle-throne corresponds precisely to the twenty-four Elders seated "round about" the throne in Revelation chapter four. I would remind the reader of the account in I Chronicles chapter twenty-four of how, under King David, the Levitical priesthood was divided into TWENTY-FOUR COURSES under the headship of TWENTY-FOUR ELDERS. The twenty-four courses or orders of the priesthood were chosen by families—according to the twenty-four grandsons of Aaron the high priest. Each course was named for one of these twenty-four grandsons and the male descendants of each grandson constituted one of the twenty-four courses through-out their generations. We are inclined to lightly pass over many profound statements of holy scripture. The priesthood was divided into twenty-four orders for this stated purpose: "This was their order for coming on duty to serve in the house of the Lord, according to the procedure ordered for them by their grandfather Aaron, as the Lord God of Israel had commanded him (1 Chronicles 24:19, AMP).

The point I wish to emphasize here is this: It took *all twenty-four courses* to *MAKE UP THE ENTIRE PRIESTHOOD OF GOD.* As the Father unfolds these truths to the inner man, we become convinced that as the four Living Creatures "in the midst of the throne" reveal the glory of KINGSHIP, so the twenty-four Elders "round about the throne" reveal the glory of PRIESTHOOD. KINGS AND PRIESTS. A KINGDOM OF PRIESTS. PRIESTS THAT SIT UPON THRONES. REIGNING PRIESTS."

Dan Luehrs

The twenty-four Elders represent the whole priesthood of God, of which Jesus is the Head, our great High Priest.

> This company of priests, reigning priests, are the twenty-four Elders round about the throne. And they sung a new song, saying, Thou hast made us unto our God kings and *priests:* and we shall reign on the earth. And I saw thrones, and they sat upon them, and... they shall be *priests of God and of Christ*, and shall reign with Him a thousand years.
>
> Revelation 20:4, 6 (NAS)

Priesthood demands suffering, trial, testing, tribulation, and pressure. *Sonship* demands relationship with God.

John the Revelator said, "And I saw thrones, and they sat upon them, and judgment was given unto them... and they shall be priests of God and of Christ, and shall reign with Him a thousand years." Here you see that it is not the sons who are reigning—it is the PRIESTS. What about the sons? "He that overcometh shall inherit all things; and I will be his God, and he shall be my son." The sons inherit, for they are heirs of God and joint-heirs with Christ (Romans 8:17). Who, then, is destined to reign? THE SONS WHO ARE PRIESTS. Christ was a Son before He was a Priest. He was not a Priest during His years in the flesh, although He was qualifying to be one, but He was a Son. Christ in His ministry from the heavens today is not merely the Son of God. As a Son He is "heir of all things." But to become the great High Priest and provide the priestly ministry on our behalf the Son had, as a Son, to go through the experience that was necessary to perfect Him for the understanding heart of the Priesthood. "We have not an High Priest which cannot be touched with the feelings of our infirmities; BUT WAS IN ALL POINTS TEMPTED LIKE AS WE ARE ..." (Hebrews 4:15). "Though He were a Son, yet learned He obedience by the things which He suffered; and being *made perfect (for the Priesthood)*, He *became*... AN HIGH PRIEST AFTER THE ORDER OF MELCHIZEDEK" (Hebrews 5:8–10). Ah, Jesus could have been a son without being so totally compassed with infirmity, BUT HE COULD NEVER HAVE BEEN A PRIEST WITHOUT IT."

The sufferings that I have been through when I have tried to obey God have made me question Him on how these things can happen to me when I only am trying to obey Him. The twenty-four divisions of priests are helping me to understand how suffering has made me to be a more compassionate person to other people's needs.

In 1995, our church experienced a true revival that changed my life and the life of many other people, but after a few months of this new move of God, some people in the church wanted to go back to "church" as it was before the move of God. The only problem was that their pastor was a changed man, and he was not going back to church as it was. What happened to me was a defining point in my life; in fact, it was the greatest event of my life. I was and still am full of the life of God, never to go back to just having church.

To make a long story short, some people began to leave the church, and then 60 percent of the people turned against me when up to that point, I had most of the people on my side helping me. But now, I was not doing as they liked, and they wanted me out so they could bring in someone that would do as they liked. Could you imagine if Moses, David, Jesus, Paul, or any of the other great leaders of the past would have done what the people wanted rather than what God wanted? Where would we be then? Lost.

Dan Luehrs

The pressure came on me so great to stop praying for people in the altars so that they would not fall under the power of God. But I knew that people were being blessed and encouraged, so how could I quit? The ministry became hard and was not fun anymore, and I wanted to leave that church and find someone, anyone, who wanted what I had to give away.

One day while I was praying about my plight, I said to God, "You must have something pretty great in heaven for us that you would allow us to go through trials like this." I was so hurt that people did not want more of God, and I would weep in the altars.

God one day said to me, "They are not rejecting you, they are rejecting me." Most of the pressure was released from me that day because there was nothing I could do for the people but pray. Years later, I now understand a little more about our high calling unto sonship and see why we need to go through what we do because we are being qualified by our perseverance under fire. Our calling is so much higher then the human mind can comprehend. Yes, it is a calling unto sonship, but it even goes much higher than that as we have seen with the living beings and now the priests of God upon the throne.

Caught up to the Throne

> After these things I looked, and behold, a door standing open in heaven [the spirit realm], and the first voice which I had heard, like the sound of a trumpet speaking with me, said, "Come up here, and I will show you what must take place after these things. Immediately I was in the Spirit; and behold, a throne was standing in heaven [the spirit realm], and One sitting on the throne.
>
> Revelation 4:1–2 (NAS)

The Lord not only invites John, but us to "come up here" by Him to be in heaven, or the spirit world through the open door that He has personally opened for us like a friend would do when we go to their house and they say, "Come on in." The Lord is not only saying, "Come on in," but "Come by me." The Lord of glory wants us to sit in the throne by Him. What an invitation!

A throne is standing in heaven. The word *standing* means "to be set or to be outstretched" in the spirit realm where God's rule and reign is. "The LORD has established [set] His throne in the heavens; and His sovereignty rules over all" (Psalms 103:19, NAS). God is now calling His church to come into the throne realm; it is open for you and me to rule and reign over our own flesh first, then to rule with Him in the kingdom. Right now, some people are caught up to the throne with Him; the question remains: will it be us, do you hear His voice calling to you, "Come up here by me"? When you hear His voice calling you, spend time with Him in His presence and let Him fill you to the brim and overflowing with Himself and with His presence on you, you will then have power to rule over self. Not only do we already sit in the heavens now, but we are also told that we can come boldly to the throne of grace each and every day. If we will come to Him and open the door of our heart, we will be caught up to be with Him, or a better phrase, raised up in Him. "And she gave birth to a son, a male child, who is to rule all the nations with a rod of iron; and her child was caught up to God and to His throne" (Revelation 12:5, NAS). We are to arise shine, and what better place to shine forth the brightness of God's glory but from the throne realm where He is manifest?

When Jacob saw God at the top of the ladder leading to heaven, Jacob was not told to climb the ladder to be with Him for it was not yet time because Jesus had not yet died for our sins so that we could be with Him. But now we have been invited to come up. If we desire to be raised up by Him, every rung on the ladder is another revelation of Jesus Christ within us; this is

Dan Luehrs

why the book of Revelation is called, "The Revelation of Jesus Christ." It is not called, "The Revelation of the End Times." Jesus is revealed in and through this book in us, and this is why we must pray for understanding about this book, for no other book promises us a blessing to understand it. We must not only know the truth of God in our heads but we must experience the truth in our heart because His word is truth and He is the Word of life; we are changed from glory to glory by it. But I must warn you that the Revelation of Jesus does not come easily or cheaply; in fact, they only come through trials and tribulations.

Trials and tribulations are doorways that we enter the kingdom of God through (Acts 14:22, NAS). Jesus tells us in Revelation 3:18 "To buy from me gold refined by fire." In other words, we are to pay the price of following Him through the fires of life, and then we will receive His nature *through* the trial. Do you remember what the gates in the New Jerusalem are made of? One giant pearl. A pearl comes about by an oyster having a stone (irritant) that becomes valuable. The entrance into the kingdom is just the same—our trials are valuable because they are paving the way and changing us.

After John the apostle opened the door of his heart to fellowship with the Master, Jesus said, "Behold, I stand at the door and knock; if anyone hears my voice and opens the door, I will come in to him, and will dine [fellowship] with him, and he with me" (Revelation 3:20, NAS). The Lord then opened the door of His throne realm for him to come up there to be with Him. Coming up is not that we leave the planet and go somewhere else, but that we come up in the spirit realm to the level where the Lord is. Notice that Jesus says He will come into us. The King is the authority (the throne), and the King lives and abides in us, and we in Him; the kingdom is within us as is the throne; we just need to get the revelation that Jesus Christ lives within us. God wants to give us the revelation of His calling, His glory, and the power of the throne *in* us. Open the door of your heart, and the King of glory will come in.

God is offering us the deal of a lifetime, or should I say eternity, and by our willingness to come to Him, He will come to us and give us His glory, which is His life—the very likeness and character of God. "The thief comes only to steal and kill and destroy; I have come that they may have life, and have it to the full" (John 10:10, NIV). God wants us to have His life to the full in us. God's glory life fills the earth, for the earth is teaming with life because God's throne is on planet earth; His life is in the plants, trees, flowers, and in every living thing. This is why so many people say they meet with God through nature because God is in nature and they are receiving His life through the life around them. Death does not give life, but life begets life, and we as humans love the feeling we get from life. It is fine for us to feel the life of God through nature, but we must go to the source of life itself, which is Jesus Christ; otherwise, we can make an idol out of the things that we receive life from. The throne realm is the very source of life; it is the fullness of life. "There was a rainbow around the throne, like an emerald in appearance" (Revelation 4:3, NAS). The rainbow around the throne was not multicolor like we see on the earth, but was one solid color, and that being green. Green is the color of life, and that is what the throne is: life, and we are to be giving this life away to all that will receive it. But if we do not have His life how will others receive? Jesus promised us eternal life because it is life eternal and all who receive it will live because God is life.

A River, a City, a Throne

A River

And he showed me a river of the water of life, clear as crystal, coming from the throne of God and of the Lamb.

Revelation 22:1 (NAS)

Dan Luehrs

To understand the book of Revelation, we must realize that the book is filled with natural symbolism to help us comprehend spiritual truth and eternal reality. Many parts of the Bible do the same thing, like in John 6:53: "Jesus therefore said to them, 'Truly, truly, I say to you, unless you eat the flesh of the Son of Man and drink His blood, you have no life in yourselves.'" Do we really eat His flesh and drink His blood in the natural? No. Yet in Psalms 34:8 the Scripture says that we are to "taste and see that the LORD is good." This "tasting" that the Word is speaking about is in our spirit man; our spirit is really who we are, and God has made it that we hunger for Him, and that which we hunger for is the throne of God because that is where the life comes from. It is God Himself that we need to live a happy and blessed life. People are looking for life in all the wrong places and things; this is why they are so devoid of true lasting life because they go from mountaintop to mountaintop. John said that he saw a river of the water of life flowing from the throne; do you really believe that there is a natural river of water flowing from the throne? Of course not; it is all typology to help us understand that true life comes from God, and a river is something we can relate to, to help us understand spiritual truth.

The real question should be: What is the life coming from the throne? I wish that I could give you a pat answer to what life is, but then I would have to tell you what God is, and I cannot do that. If I were to explain life, I would use the analogy of electricity because it is unseen and it is powerful, and the only thing John could liken life to in his day was a river of water. If we see a sparking power line down, we would call it a "live wire" because it has power flowing through it. On many occasions, I have put my hand on a person's head, and I could feel electricity flowing from my hand into his head when they were receiving the life or power of God. Jesus said in Mark 5:30, "And immediately Jesus, perceiving in Himself that the power proceeding from Him had gone forth, turned around in the crowd and said, 'Who touched my garments?'" God's life is the power for living life on earth that people are looking for in many other places and in things and are not finding it there because it can only be found in the person of Jesus Christ. In John 14:6, Jesus clearly said that He is life and we cannot get it any other way but through Him.

Medical science teaches us that we have an electrical system in our body that keep the heart and mind in perfect rhythm. We have got to have this electric pulse in us, or we die; and one thing I know for sure is that we can tell when life is not. When a person stops breathing, we say that he is dead; or when we go to a church service and the presence of God is not there, we say that it was dead. What we are really saying is that there was not any life there. In the beginning, God breathed the breath of life into man; life originates from God. To understand life, we must understand that God is life, it comes from Him, He does not create life because He is life, and if we want true life, we must go to Him daily. John the apostle said that life is like a river of water—this is to give us understanding that we need spiritual life like we need natural water; in order for us to be truly happy, we must drink God's life in every day.

Life is to flow from our heart; that is where the throne is. "Keep your heart with all diligence, for out of it spring the issues of life" (Proverbs 4:23, NKJV). "For the mouth speaks out of that which fills the heart" (Matthew 12:34, NAS). If we desire to give God's life away to others, we must learn how to speak from our heart and not just from the head. Head knowledge brings death unto the hearers; Jesus spoke as no other man because He spoke with great authority from the heart, and all His enemies knew it. The anointing is the life of God that flows through our words; His river of life is released through us by speaking to one another from the heart. Oh, God, teach us how to speak from our heart and to give Your life away, so that others might benefit and be strengthened in You. Amen.

Dan Luehrs

A City

And I saw the holy city, new Jerusalem, coming down out of heaven from God, made ready as a bride adorned for her husband.

Revelation 21:2 (NAS)

Come here, I shall show you the bride, the wife of the Lamb. And he carried me away in the Spirit to a great and high mountain, and showed me the holy city, Jerusalem, coming down out of heaven from God.

Revelation 21:9–10 (NAS)

Very clearly John sees the New Jerusalem coming down from the spirit realm into the natural realm. This city is the body and bride of Jesus Christ. John uses many analogies in this chapter to try to explain how wonderful and glorious this bride really is; when reading about the city, we must always remember that it is a body of people, not bricks and mortar. God is building a city made out of living stones: "You also, as living stones, are being built up as a spiritual house for a holy priesthood, to offer up spiritual sacrifices acceptable to God through Jesus Christ" (1 Peter 2:5, NAS). We are His tabernacle or dwelling place that He will manifest Himself through to all the people of the earth and wipe away every tear and heal all the nations, and there will be no more death. Hallelujah! This is what we are called to: to be the holy priesthood that God will minister through to all the people of the earth. What a calling, what a future, and what a hope.

In whom the whole building, being fitted together is growing into a holy temple in the Lord; in whom you also are being built together into a dwelling of God in the Spirit.

Ephesians 2:21–22 (NAS)

Do you not know that you are a temple of God, and that the Spirit of God dwells in you?

1 Corinthians 3:16 (NAS)

Individually we are a temple of God, but God is building something much bigger that we are a part of; it is the tabernacle of God that comes down from God to the earth—it is a city, it is a tabernacle, and it is God in His people.

> And I heard a loud voice from the throne, saying, "Behold, the tabernacle of God is among men, and He shall dwell among them, and they shall be His people, and God Himself shall be among them."

Revelation 21:3 (NAS)

You and I, the body of Christ, are the great tabernacle that God is building and will one day manifest Himself on the earth to change mankind. "For the anxious longing of the creation waits eagerly for the revealing of the sons of God" (Romans 8:19, NAS). The earth is waiting to be delivered from sin and death.

A Throne

> And there shall no longer be any curse; and the throne of God and of the Lamb shall be in it [the city], and His bond-servants shall serve Him.

Revelation 22:3 (NAS)

When John saw the river of life flowing from the throne, he was still writing about the city—the New Jerusalem. The living water was flowing from the bride where the throne of God is, God is in His people, and His throne is where He is. God's life will flow from us as Jesus said in John 7:38: "He who believes in me, as the Scripture said, From his innermost being shall flow rivers of liv-

Dan Luehrs

ing water." Jesus is talking about His life flowing from us so that we can give it away to the nations while we rule and reign with Him on earth for His life is in us.

> And they shall see His face, and His name shall be on their foreheads. And there shall no longer be any night; and they shall not have need of the light of a lamp nor the light of the sun, because the Lord God shall illumine them; and they shall reign forever and ever. And he said to me, "These words are faithful and true…"
>
> Revelation 22:4–6 (NAS)

His word is faithful and true—believe it.

The Cross,
the Message,
the Ministry

The Message

Then He said to them all, "If anyone desires to come after Me, *let him deny himself, and take up his cross daily, and follow Me.* For whoever desires to save his life will lose it, but whoever loses his life for My sake will save it.

Luke 9:23–24, NKJV

If your desire is to be a true follower of Jesus Christ, an overcomer, then there is only one method that has the power to break the stronghold of sin in your life—*the cross*. There are two crosses, one that Jesus died on for us, and one that that we die on to gain Christ's likeness over the power of sin. Jesus gave His all for His bride; the Father is expecting us to give our all to be joint-heirs with His Son. Romans 12:1 says, "…That you present *your bodies a living sacrifice*, holy, acceptable to God, which is your reasonable service." Why is giving of ourselves a reasonable service to God? Because Jesus paid the price to give us His all, His life for our life! Jesus paid the ultimate price for us, so why should we not have to pay the ultimate price for Him? This is our reasonable service to God!

I have not endeavored to write about our personal cross, which we are called to carry. One reason is because I have not understood much of it nor have I felt the need to write about it. The message of the cross is not a very popular message in our day or should I say in anyone's day! Who really wants to hear about self-denial and carring a cross anyway? I do, the overcomers do, in fact they rejoice in the cross because it gives them more of what they love the most—Jesus! My greatest desire is to be one with my Lord and to share His glory, which we have been invited too, but unless we are willing to suffer with Him we will not be glorified with Him. We must come to know Him through the fellowship of His suffering and to be conformed to His death. I do not speak of physical death here, but rather, death to the man of sin living inside of us that is trying to turn us from following Jesus wherever He wants us to go in life. Living our life on the cross is about total self-denial and obeying the leading of Jesus rather than doing what we want to do in life. This is how we become overcomers!

The key to dying to self is, "Take up his cross daily, and follow Me!" To obediently follow Jesus each day is the cross we are called to bare; the cross is being worked in our life so that we will come forth with His likeness and character. Only the cross can do this, so for us to fight against it would be pure foolishness if we desire to be overcomers! Think about it, the more we are

Dan Luehrs

around certain people, the more we will begin to act like them. In order for us to become an overcomer we must follow the only true overcomer that finished His course so that we may become like Him. "These are the ones who follow the Lamb wherever He goes" (Rev. 14:4). When we follow the great Overcomer, we too will become overcomers through the training that He gives us; through this process of the cross the way of our flesh will be shaken to the core of who we are. Our job description is to walk with Him daily in obedience as He leads us. The Holy Spirit will always lead us in the way of the cross that is opposed to our flesh so that we might be crucified. If you are looking for ease in your Christian life stop and ask yourself, "Where is the cross in this that I am seeking after?" Our culture is looking for quick and easy way to do everything, but there is no easy way to carry a cross because it is meant to kill us. We are called to be a living sacrifice!

We hear so very little about the sacrificing of ourselves to God because we are so busy trying to save ourselves from pain and looking foolish in the eyes of others. It was on the cross (humility) that Jesus publicly defeated the devil and it is on our cross that we too will defeat the power of our flesh! "[God] disarmed the principalities and powers that were ranged against us and made a bold display and public example of them, in triumphing over them in Him and in it [the cross]" (Col 2:15, AMP). The cross of Christ is what brought down the power of the enemy and our cross will do likewise for us if we surrender our all to God and die to self, rather than fighting against the crosses that He sends us. Satan is a defeated foe and we must enforce the laws that have already been written against him by submitting to our cross, which is the instrument of our victory over him.

When we sacrifice our all to God and are dying to ourselves, we are gaining Christ and that is what true life is all about! The more we give of ourselves to Him, the more God gives of Himself to us, the more we empty ourselves of all our worldliness the faster God will fill us with His glory. "For our light affliction, which is but for a moment, *is working for us a far more exceeding and eternal weight of glory*" (2 Corinthians 4:17 NKJV). Our sacrificing to God does not cause us to become poorer, but richer in the things of Christ; this is the purpose of the cross in our lives, so rejoice in it because you are rich! This is why the Paul apostle could say that he rejoiced in the cross that crucified him to the world and gave him more of Jesus, and once we see this, we too will gain more of Christ. "But God forbid that I should boast except in the cross of our Lord Jesus Christ, by whom the world has been crucified to me, and I to the world" (Galatians 6:14, NKJV). The Christian life is about death to self and life in Christ, *the cross that we are called to carry causes death to come to the man of sin in us, delivering death unto our death.* Oh the wisdom of God in the power of the cross!

> The great Chinese writer Watchman Nee wrote about the cross in his book, *The Normal Christian Life*, on page 26 he says, "The blood can wash away my sins, but it cannot wash away my 'old man.' It needs the Cross to crucify me. The blood deals with the sins, but the Cross must deal with the sinner."

If our greatest desire is to know Jesus in His fullness and to be an overcomer we will each have to identify with His cross of suffering through our life-time. "And they that are Christ's have crucified the flesh with the affections and lusts" (Gal 5:24, KJV). The word affection here means, "Suffering, pain, hardships." Lust means, "A longing for that which is forbidden." This is my interpretation of this verse, "Those who belong to Christ have put to death their sin by daily bearing their cross through their sufferings and pains of the cravings of the flesh." All human beings suffer, but suffering does not have to be in vain, God wants us to use the pain of the cross for our redemption from the power of the flesh.

Dan Luehrs

The cross we are called to carry will deliver us from the power of sin that has held us in bondage as we obey Him, but when we chose to disobey, He will allow tribulations to come into our life so that we might be disciplined as a child. "Now no chastening seems to be joyful for the present, but painful; nevertheless, afterward it yields the peaceable fruit of righteousness to those who have been trained by it" (Hebrews 12:11, NKJV). The training and obedience of the cross is very painful for the moment to our flesh, but it will bring forth a peaceable fruit of righteousness into our life, which is the fruit of Christ.

Understanding the Cross

When I first began to understand my life lived on the cross it seemed like a wasted life to me and to those around me because I was going through a breaking process that killed my pride. God wants the pride of life to be dead in us through our obedience to Him in faith. It takes great faith to overcome the sins of the flesh like, fear, doubt, and unbelief and to follow the Lord when it looks so foolish to us and others. "Through Him we have received grace and apostleship for obedience to the faith among all nations for His name" (Romans 1:5, NKJV). Obedience is the key to true faith working in us. What does obedience look like; does it mean that I will have to move to Africa? It may if God calls you there! In a truer sense it means that I obey the small promptings in my heart like, not to say bad things about other people or even to think evil of them, but to love them. It may mean to bless our enemies with a glass of water or just a smile when we really want to tell them off. One of the greatest tests of obedience that we can pass is to spend time with the Lord each day when our flesh would rather do something else to satisfy it. We bring great joy to the heart of God when we take time to be with Him and what true Christian would not want to give joy to their heavenly Father?

The message of the cross is to die to self so that we may lose our own life, to gain His life. "For what profit is it to a man if he gains the whole world, and loses his own soul? Or what will a man give in exchange for his soul? For the Son of Man will come in the glory of His Father with His angels, and then *He will reward each according to his works*" (Matthew 16:26–27, NKJV). When Jesus returns, His reward will be with Him, which is His eternal life, the manifest presence of His likeness to those who have been faithful. To those who have given up their life to follow the Lamb wherever He goes will receive His life and likeness. Please listen to what the Bible says, "For what profit is it to a man if he gains the whole world, and loses his own soul?" What this is saying to me is, what good would it do for us to have everything in this world, but we miss out on the eternal life of Jesus for ourselves? The Father has promised those who follow Jesus the kingdom and its true riches for eternity. Oh yes, it will be worth it all to follow Him as we take up our cross daily!

The cross is what kills the flesh so that Jesus can break forth from us. The life of Jesus is hidden deep inside of our earth, in the hard husk of our flesh and when our husk is broken by the cross His life is then able to break forth from us into the lives of others. God is shaking everything that can be shaken out of our lives so that only Jesus will remain inside of us with no works of our flesh remaining. Without the working of the cross in our daily life we will block much of the life of Jesus from others to see Him in us. In fact, if we do not have the dying of Jesus working in us we cannot have His life either! "Always carrying about in the body the dying (the cross) of the Lord Jesus, that the life of Jesus also may be manifested in our body" (2 Corinthians 4:10, NKJV). We love the glory of His presence, but we hate the pressure of the cross and this too must change, to where we love our cross, so that we can share His life with others.

When we learn to love the fire of the cross is when we know that it is for the purpose of us gaining the glory of the Lord. And

Dan Luehrs

as we begin to glory in the cross we will again see the resurrection power of God flowing through the church. "And for me, let it not be—to glory, except in the cross of our Lord Jesus Christ, through which to me the world hath been crucified, and I to the world" (Galatians 6:14, YLT). The ways of the world will have been crucified to us and we will know that we are becoming more like Christ. This is the reason why we should rejoice in the working of the cross in our life so that He may shine forth through us. This is the message of the cross we must carry! "For the message of the cross is foolishness to those who are perishing, but to us who are being saved it is the power of God" (1 Corinthians 1:18, NKJV). To live the life of the cross is pure foolishness to the carnal man, but for us who are being saved it is the power of God working in our life. Being saved means that there is the process of the cross that we all must go through to be stripped of self.

Do you want the power of God working in your life? Then rejoice in the cross that God has allowed in your life to crucify the man of sin. Our cross means death to self so that the life and power of Christ may come forth. Why is the cross foolishness then? Because it absolutely makes no sense whatsoever to the natural mind! Our mind wants to know why we are suffering and then we try to figure it all out, thinking that God must be mad at us or something, but God wants us to *trust* in His goodness in our life. The cross is the very thing that is bringing the power of God into our life so that we may partake of His glory, yet we fight against the cross that He sends us.

> "And He said to me, 'My grace is sufficient for you, for My strength is made perfect in weakness.' *Therefore most gladly I will rather boast in my infirmities* (The cross), *that the power of Christ may rest upon me*" (2 Cor 12:9, NKJV).

Paul was going though one of the most difficult times in his life when Jesus told him that His grace was sufficient for the cross that he was carrying in his life. Paul then began to understand that his weaknesses were being replaced by the strength of God in his life. He could then say, "Therefore I take pleasure in infirmities, in reproaches, in needs, in persecutions, in distresses, for Christ's sake. For when I am weak, then I am strong" (verse 10). Have you come to the point of taking pleasure in your cross? I am still working on that one! When we begin to rejoice in our trials, we will then see the power of Christ resting upon our lives and the ministry that we have been called to. Our suffering releases the power of God upon our weaknesses. Jesus embraced the humiliation of His cross because He knew this truth and was given a name above all names because of it. We too must embrace our days of humiliation if we are going to sit in the throne with Him. The way of the cross is humility and this is normal Christianity; we must learn to glory in the cross that He sends us, for it is God's only method to make us overcomers.

The Ministry

> And I, brethren, if I still preach circumcision (the law), why do I still suffer persecution? *Then the offense of the cross has ceased.*
>
> Galatians 5:11 (NKJV)

When Paul was a Pharisee he preached a message of circumcision under the law, which brought him no persecution, but when his message changed to the cross of Christ he was persecuted nonstop by the religious horde. Today the message of the cross is offensive to both the saved and unsaved. Why is that? The unsaved cannot believe in a two-thousand-year-old story about a man dying on a cross because it is foolishness to their mind. To the saved person, even though they have come to know Jesus

Dan Luehrs

through the blood of His cross they do not understand the cross that they have been called to carry everyday, in fact they run from it!

Here is what I see the problem is, those of us who are in the ministry do not preach or live the cross of Christ that will bring great trials and persecutions to our life. From the beginning those who have preached the gospel have suffered persecution and those in many parts of the world still suffer for preaching the cross, but not in the West. The ministry itself was meant to be costly, and as we stay on the cross the power of God will flow through us; this is the reason why we see so many more miracles in other countries than we do in the West. The Spirit of God led Jesus to the desert and to the cross, the Spirit also led Paul to a place of suffering and arrested in Jerusalem, the Spirit also brought John to the Island of Patmos to suffer tribulation. The Holy Spirit will always lead us to the cross where we are called to die to self. If most preachers are persecuted for their message they will change it and preach a message to the itching ears of the people. But in order for ministers to preach the cross, *they must live the cross!* This is in total opposition of what most preachers are living today because they want a life of ease and comfort. In most churches the ministry is no different from any other profession and is very well compensated for their overseeing the work of the church. But they have very little power in their ministry to see the lives of people affected and changed. They desire a nice comfortable office, home, cars, and large pay checks to show the world and themselves how successful they are, but it was not this way in the beginning. Worldly things are not going to bring people to Christ! We must live the cross if we are going to preach the cross and see the lives of people changed around us!

David Wilkerson wrote the following e-mail devotional and was sent to me on April 14, 2009, after I had finished writing on the cross. I felt like the Lord was confirming to me that I had the right message for our time.

No one on earth can place you in ministry. You may be given a diploma by a seminary, ordained by a bishop, or commissioned by a denomination. But the apostle Paul reveals the only source of any true call to ministry: "I thank Christ Jesus our Lord, who hath enabled me, for that he counted me faithful, putting me into the ministry" (1 Timothy 1:12).

What does Paul mean here when he says Jesus enabled him and counted him faithful? Think back to the apostle's conversion. Three days after that event, Christ placed Paul in the ministry—specifically, the ministry of suffering: "For I will shew him how great things he must suffer for my name's sake" (Acts 9:16). This is the very ministry Paul refers to when he says, "Therefore seeing we have this ministry ..." (2 Corinthians 4:1). He continues, adding, "... as we have received mercy, we faint not." He's talking about the ministry of suffering. And he makes clear it is a ministry that we all have.

Paul is telling us Jesus gave him a promise for this ministry. Christ pledged to remain faithful to him and enable him through all his trials. The Greek word for *enabled* means "a continual supply of strength." Paul declares, "Jesus promised to give me more than sufficient strength for the journey. He enables me to remain faithful in this ministry. Because of him, I won't faint or give in. I'll emerge with a testimony."

A transfiguration is taking place in all our lives. The truth is, we're being changed by what obsesses us. We're becoming like the things that occupy our minds. Our character is being influenced and impacted by whatever has hold of our hearts.

I thank God for everyone who feeds his mind and soul with spiritual things. Such servants have fixed their eyes on what is pure and holy. They keep their gaze fixed on Christ, spending quality time worshipping him and

Dan Luehrs

building themselves up in faith. The Holy Spirit is at work in these saints, continually changing their character in Christ's. These believers will be ready for the hard, explosive sufferings to come. Slothful, lazy, prayerless believers will suffer heart failure or breakdowns. They'll be crushed by their fears, because they don't have the Holy Spirit at work in them, transfiguring them. When the hard times come, they simply won't make it.

Here is Paul's final word on the matter: "Giving no offence in anything, that the ministry be not blamed: but in all things approving ourselves as the ministers of God, in much patience, in afflictions, in necessities, in distresses, in stripes, in imprisonment's.... As sorrowful, yet always rejoicing; as poor, yet making many rich" (2 Corinthians 6:3–5, 10). How do we "make many rich"? By outshining the hope of Christ in the midst of our sufferings. We offer true riches when we cause others to ask, "What's his secret? Where does he find such peace?" (End of quote).

The Price of Ministry

The Bible verses below are what I call, Paul's Manifesto for Ministry. After you finish reading the price of true ministry ask yourself if you really want to be a messenger of the cross.

> For I think that God has displayed us, *the apostles, last,* as men condemned to death; for *we have been made a spectacle to the world, both to angels and to men.* We are fools for Christ's sake, but you are wise in Christ! We are weak, but you are strong! You are distinguished, but we are dishonored! To the present hour we both hunger and thirst, and we are poorly clothed, and beaten, and homeless. And we labor, working with our own hands.

Being reviled, we bless; being persecuted, we endure; being defamed, we entreat. *We have been made as the filth of the world, the offscouring of all things until now.*

1 Corinthians 4:9–13 (NKJV)

But in all things we commend ourselves as ministers of God: in much patience, in tribulations, in needs, in distresses, in stripes, in imprisonments, in tumults, in labors, in sleeplessness, in fastings; by purity, by knowledge, by longsuffering, by kindness, by the Holy Spirit, by sincere love, by the word of truth, by the power of God, by the armor of righteousness on the right hand and on the left, by honor and dishonor, by evil report and good report; as deceivers, and yet true; as unknown, and yet well known; as dying, and behold we live; as chastened, and yet not killed; as sorrowful, yet always rejoicing; as poor, yet making many rich; *as having nothing, and yet possessing all things.*

2 Corinthians 6:4–10 (NKJV)

Now after reading those stunning words about the ministry listen to what else Paul tells us to do, "Therefore *I urge you, imitate me*" (1 Corinthians 4:16, NKJV). What are you saying, Paul? Do you want us to imitate you and suffer like you and our Lord? Yes! We may not be called to do the ministry like Paul did, but we are called to follow the Lord wherever He may lead us and this is sure to cause our flesh much suffering. Now I ask you again, do you really want this New Testament ministry for your life's calling and to go wherever He sends you? When the apostles suffered for the name of Jesus they rejoiced that they were worthy to suffer for His name, and we too must come to this point in our life if we really desire to do the work of the ministry with power.

That no one should be shaken by these afflictions; for you yourselves know that we are appointed to this. For, in fact, we told you before when we were with you that we would suffer tribulation, just as it happened, and you know. For this reason, when I could no longer endure it, I sent to know your faith, lest by some means the tempter had tempted you, and our labor might be in vain.

1 Thessalonians 3:3–5 (NKJV)

Paul had a powerful ministry because he lived and preached the power of the cross. The life that he lived was foolishness to the church, the Pharisees, and to the Roman world of his day; they all thought he had gone mad. Yet Jesus was faithfully right by his side leading and guiding him along the way. The sufferings that we are called to go through with the Lord are not desired by most Christian's because they see no essential value in suffering, they do not understand what suffering is doing for their spirit man. Some of the things that the Lord may call us to might seem so minuscule and so humbling to our flesh that we think there is no way that God would call us to such a thing. Take Paul for instance, he had his doctorate in the Law of God and was taught by the best of the best and yet we find him making tents to survive and going hungry at times. How could God allow this to happen to this great man of learning? This is because God is not a respecter of man's person! Paul then called all this stuff dung compared to the knowledge of Jesus Christ.

When God called me to move to Florida from South Dakota I thought for sure the Lord would open for me a great door of ministry because I gave my church up to follow Him. Then one day God told me to take a driving job and I said this cannot be your will for me? He said, "Have you not prayed for My will to be done in your life?" "Yes I did, but this cannot be your will for me to leave ministry and drive a truck!" He replied, "It is." Through my obedience He showed me the next phase of ministry for me to do. God is working His will in our life if we will just trust Him to carry it out.

The ministry is not what we might think it is; it's not for us to make a name for ourselves, for only the Lord can receive the glory and not stumble because of pride. So He allows trials and tribulations in our life to cause us to stay humble. We are not to become rich with earthly things from the ministry, but we can become rich in Christ throughout eternity. When we begin to rejoice in our suffering is when God will entrust us with greater trials and will unlock the revelation of Jesus Christ into our life, and this will cause us to become more Christ like.

> *I now rejoice in my sufferings for you*, and fill up in my flesh what is lacking in the afflictions of Christ, for the sake of His body, which is the church, of which I became a minister according to the stewardship from God which was given to me for you, to fulfill the word of God, the mystery which has been hidden from ages and from generations, but now has been revealed to His saints. To them God willed to make known what are the riches of the glory of this mystery among the Gentiles: which is Christ in you, the hope of glory. Him we preach, warning every man and teaching every man in all wisdom, that we may present every man perfect in Christ Jesus. To this end I also labor, striving according to His working which works in me mightily.
>
> Colossians 1:24–29 (NKJV)

Dan Luehrs

Every Eye Will See Him

Blessed is he who reads and those who hear the words of the prophecy, and heed the things which are written in it; for the time is near.

Revelation 1:3 (NAS)

Most evangelical believers know this verse quite well because they have heard much preaching on the book of Revelation and how it pertains to the end times. Yet we never seem to tie verse 3 and 4 together so that we might receive more of a blessing from God on understanding this book. Verse 4 reads, "John to the seven churches that are in Asia: Grace to you and peace, from Him who is and who was and who is to come; and from the seven Spirits who are before His throne." Yes, there is a great blessing to those that read and understand this book because they have been given the mysteries of the unveiling of Jesus Christ. Jesus said in Matthew 13:11, "To you it has been granted to know the mysteries of the kingdom of heaven, but to them it has not been granted." The book of Revelation opens the way of our understanding on how Jesus is to manifest Himself through us. This book is not about the destruction of the nations but the destruction of the man of sin that abides in us. Then Jesus can fully abide in us through the death of self. To the degree that we die to self, He will be fully manifested in us. If we choose not to go through or complete the death process, we will end up being the loser.

The great blessing of verse 4 is "Grace to you and peace, from Him." With God's grace, we have His strength and peace so that we can go through anything God requires of us in this death process. This whole thing that we call life is a setup by God so we will die to self; then He can fill us with all His fullness. "And He has said to me, 'My grace is sufficient for you, for power is perfected in weakness.' Most gladly, therefore, I will rather boast about my weaknesses, that the power of Christ may dwell in me" (2 Corinthians 12:9, NAS). It is in our weakness that His grace begins to kick in to help us. Much like how adrenaline works in the body, it kicks in when we're under great pressure to help keep us going. If we are going on into the fullness of God, we will have a great need for the grace of God to keep us on the right path to Him.

The Patience of Jesus Christ

I, John, both your brother and companion in the tribulation and kingdom and patience of Jesus Christ, was on the island that is called Patmos for the word of God and for the testimony of Jesus Christ.

Revelation 1:9, NKJV

Here is the patience of the saints; here are those who keep the commandments of God and the faith of Jesus.

Revelation 14:12, NKJV

Dan Luehrs

The sign of great tribulation in your life is not a sign of God's displeasure with you but is possibly a sign of God's approval on your life because you are worthy to suffer for His name. (See 2 Thessalonians 1:5.) The man named Christian in *The Pilgrim's Progress* said, "For their [our] present deliverance, they do not much expect it: but, *they stay for their glory, and they shall have it,* when their Prince comes *in* His, and the glory of the angels." Our tribulations are only preparing us for His glory to fill us so that Jesus will be manifested through us.

John said that he was their companion in *the* tribulation. He didn't say in the tribulation that is coming but that *is*. We also will have tribulation in our life, and we should be thankful for it because it is preparing us to receive the kingdom of God. Acts 14:22 says, "Strengthening the souls of the disciples, encouraging them to continue in the faith, and saying, 'Through many tribulations we must enter the kingdom of God.'" I ask you, if it takes tribulation for us to enter into the fullness of God, why are we always complaining about it then? Perhaps we might be thinking that we did something wrong and God is mad at us; or that we have missed Him in something, so we are being punished, even as our parents punished us for doing something wrong. This is why John called it the patience of Jesus Christ because we have to patiently suffer through many trials with perseverance without knowing why. The word *patience* means for us to stay under our tribulation until God brings us the deliverance that we want in His timing.

> And after you have suffered for a little while, the God of all grace, who called you to His eternal glory in Christ, will Himself perfect, confirm, strengthen and establish you.
>
> 1 Peter 5:10, NAS

God has called us to eternal glory? This is not about us simply going to heaven, but that we are sharers of His glory, which is the essence of who He is. It is after we have suffered a little while that He will bring our deliverance according to the will of God.

> Therefore, let those also who suffer according to the will of God entrust their souls to a faithful Creator in doing what is right.
>
> 1 Peter 4:19 (NAS)

Yes, it is God's will for us to suffer in this lifetime so that we might be emptied of self and filled with God. Every true Christian who has ever served Christ went through great trials, and it will not be any different for us if we too want to gain the prize of His high calling. In fact, it was only the two churches in the book of Revelation who were suffering that were pleasing God.

> Do not fear what you are about to suffer. Behold, the devil is about to cast some of you into prison, that you may be tested, and you will have tribulation ten days. Be faithful until death, and I will give you the crown of life.
>
> Revelation 2:10 (NAS)

So it is in our trials that we too can be pleasing to God by staying faithful to what He has already shown us. Without faith, it is impossible to please God, and faith is what we must contend for when we are in the fires of life because true faith is more precious than gold to God.

To See the Voice

> I was in the Spirit on the Lord's day, and I heard behind me a loud voice like the sound of a trumpet.
>
> Revelation 1:10, NAS

Dan Luehrs

John heard a voice when he was in the Spirit on the Lord's day, but this was not just any given Sunday on the calendar as some would have us suppose. John was spiritually and prophetically seeing the terrible day of the Lord when Jesus comes with the saints to judge the man of sin through His church. (See Jude 14, 15.)

The loud voice said:

> Saying, "I am the Alpha and the Omega, the First and the Last," and, "What you see, write in a book and send it to the seven churches which are in Asia: to Ephesus, to Smyrna, to Pergamos, to Thyatira, to Sardis, to Philadelphia, and to Laodicea."
>
> Revelation 1:11 (NKJV)

Four times in the first chapter of the book of Revelation God gives His credentials by saying who and what He is. (See verses 4, 8, 11, 17–18.) Now why would the almighty God have to give His credentials to us four times in such a small book? God is trying to drive home a point that we should not miss. The point is this: He is God, and we had better take heed to what He is saying to the church through this book if we want to receive the reward of the overcomer. Through this book, we will be blessed and prepared for the high calling of God. Revelation starts with the directive to the church, not to the world, and then it ends with the church in Revelation 22:16. The whole theme of this book is about Jesus receiving His bride in His likeness so that He might be revealed through her. Notice in the verse above that God is partially speaking to the seven churches, which are in Asia, but He is also speaking to the church throughout the whole span of time on earth. He is speaking to us loud and clear.

John now turns to see the voice, but there's a problem. We cannot see a voice, but can only hear one. However, we can see where a voice is coming from. Take notice from what John sees first and where the voice is coming from: "And I turned to see the voice that was speaking with me. And having turned I saw seven golden lampstands" (Revelation 1:12, NAS). But wait—who and what are the lampstands? They are the seven churches that represent the matured church, made and fashioned into the likeness of Jesus through their tribulations. (See verse 20.) Ephesians 4:13 says, "Until we all attain to the unity of the faith, and of the knowledge of the Son of God, to a mature man, to the measure of the stature which belongs to the fullness of Christ." We must know that the church is called to be like Jesus. He took the time in this book to rebuke or praise the seven churches (us) on where they were in their walk with Him. To each one of these churches, He gave great promises of eternal rewards to those who would overcome in this life. This is why our lives are so difficult. We have been given such a high calling to overcome all that God allows in our lifetime.

John received a wonderful revelation from the Lord in typology on what the church is called to be: light, even as God is. A lampstand lights the way for others to see the truth.

> And in the middle of the lampstands one like a son of man, clothed in a robe reaching to the feet, and girded across His breast with a golden girdle.
>
> Revelation 1:13 (NAS)

John sees one *like* the Son of man standing in the middle of the church. Even as Jesus lives in the middle of each one of us, so He's in the middle of His true church when He speaks. The church is called to be His prophet that He speaks through. Notice how John says that He is "like" the Son of man. When we use the word *like,* we are comparing something that looks similar to something else. For instance, the Holy Spirit is *like* rain, water, oil, etc., but He is not them. I believe what John is saying is: "I see what seems to resemble Jesus standing in the midst of the church." John said that He was *like* the Son of man because His

Dan Luehrs

body was covered with a garment down to His feet. John couldn't see His face to identify Him for certain. I am sure that this is just how God wants His true body to be—incognito—so that no one can receive the glory other than Jesus alone because the church is called to be *like* the Son of man.

Shoulder to Shoulder

And the sons of the Levites carried the ark of God on their shoulders, with the poles thereon as Moses had commanded according to the word of the LORD.

1 Chronicles 15:15 (NAS)

Not one single person makes up the body of Christ. We are all individual members of it so that we might work together as one identity in Jesus. One person alone could not have carried the ark of God, for it represents the glory and authority of God. It took a prepared group of people to move it. Likewise, this is saying to our generation that His body will be in oneness to carry the glory of God on their shoulders, just how God gave Moses the pattern for it to be carried thousands of years ago. The name *Levi* means "unity," and that is what the body Christ will have one day on this earth so that they can carry the glory of the Lord into the entire world. "And the glory which Thou hast given me I have given to them; that they may be one, just as we are one" (John 17:22, NAS). Some years ago, I saw a vision of people marching in rank shoulder to shoulder to do the work of God in unity. Even though I had a limited understanding of what it meant, I now see that it is a corporate body ministry that He will return in, to fulfill the coming of the Lord Jesus Christ. After this vision, God gave me Zephaniah 3:9 to confirm what I saw: "For then I will give to the peoples purified lips, that all of them may call on the name of the LORD, to serve Him shoulder to shoulder" (NAS). The government and authority of God will rest upon the shoulders of His sons (Isaiah 9:6, NAS). You might say that this is Jesus alone, and it is; but when we begin to understand that He will be appearing through His body, which is His son and bride, then we can understand who He will rule through.

A Purified People

> And His feet were like burnished bronze, when it has been caused to glow in a furnace, and His voice was like the sound of many waters.
>
> Revelation 1:15 (NAS)

The body of Jesus has lips and feet that are purified even as Zephaniah 3:9 prophesied them to be: "For then I will give to the peoples purified lips." Their lips represent their speech. Their feet represent their walk and how God has brought them through the judgment of carrying their cross daily to kill the self-nature in each one of them. The body will be a pure and spotless bride that will be ready for Him to come through. (See Revelation 19:7–8.) And it is through the furnace of affliction that we are being prepared for His calling. Malachi 3:2–3 says:

> But who can endure the day of His coming? And who can stand when He appears? For He is like a refiner's fire and like fullers' soap. And He will sit as a smelter and purifier of silver, and He will purify the sons of Levi [those you will carry the glory] and refine them like gold and silver, so that they may present to the LORD offerings in righteousness.

Because these people have been prepared through the fires of God, they now have purified lips so they can speak for Him even

Dan Luehrs

as Isaiah had his lips purified in Isaiah 6 as a sign that he was cleansed. Our destiny is to be clean and holy.

> And His head and His hair were white like white wool, like snow; and His eyes were like a flame of fire.
>
> Revelation 1:14 (NAS)

John was trying to drive a point home here that His hair was pure white, like snow. White in the Scriptures represents purity and holiness. This is the representative of what covers the mind of the body of Christ—purity. They are a people that are freed from the sinful carnal nature of man.

When the church has been purified in spirit, soul, and body, they will then have the authority to speak as the voice of many waters (Revelation 1:15, NASV). Once again we see the voice that spoke with John like a trumpet. But this time, it sounded like many waters. The voice of many waters is the many membered body of Christ speaking in unity the Word of God, the sword of the Spirit. Then the gospel of the kingdom will be preached to all nations.

> And in His right hand He held seven stars; and out of His mouth came a sharp two-edged sword; and His face was like the sun shining in its strength.
>
> Revelation 1:16 (NAS)

Notice how His face was not seen, but somehow John knew that it was the Lord. The nations will know that it is Jesus in this face-less body because He said in Matthew 13:43, "Then the righteous will shine forth as the sun in the kingdom of their Father. He who has ears, let him hear."

The Nations Will See and Mourn

And when I saw Him, I fell at His feet as a dead man.
And He laid His right hand upon me, saying, "Do not
be afraid; I am the first and the last."

Revelation 1:17 (NAS)

When John saw Jesus in the midst of His people with such glory, he fell at His feet as a dead man. Even though John saw Jesus several times after His resurrection and even had lunch with Him on the beach, he never fell at His feet as a dead man that we know of. How much more will the nations mourn and fall at His feet in repentance for their lives lived in sin, ignorance, and idolatry when they see Jesus coming in His people with great power and glory: "Behold, He is coming with the clouds [His cloud of witnesses], and every eye will see Him, even those who pierced Him; and all the tribes of the earth will mourn over Him. Even so. Amen" (Revelation 1:7, NAS). They will see Him when He comes in His tens of thousands of believers that have lived with the patience of Jesus Christ and have come through with His likeness and glory. Our bodies are made for the glory of God, and we were created in His likeness to manifest Him through our bodies. Even at this time, we are carrying about the life and dying of Jesus in our bodies (2 Corinthians 4:10, NAS). You, my friend, have a part in the body of Christ's, so do not be overly concerned about the fiery trials that try you, for they are preparing you for His glory.

Dan Luehrs

The Full Measurement of Christ

Until we all attain to the unity of the faith, and of the knowledge of the Son of God, to a mature [complete, finished] man, to the measure of the stature, which belongs to the fullness of Christ. But speaking the truth in love, we are to grow up in all aspects into Him, who is the head, even Christ.

Ephesians 4:13, 15 (NAS)

As a child, I had a goal of one day growing up to be an adult. In fact, I would say, "When I grow up, I am going to do this or that." Yet, today as an adult, I still have a goal of growing up; not my physical body, but my spirit man to grow into the likeness of Jesus, manifesting His glory and life to a world that is dead. When we look at ourselves in our present condition, then look at how Jesus lived, we could get quite discouraged and wonder how we could ever come into the full likeness of Him. However, we need to understand that we cannot change ourselves into His likeness, but that God's working *in us* to bring about the change. Yes, it looks impossible, but our God is the God of impossibilities. Some say that salvation is the greatest miracle God can do for us, but I think that making us into the likeness of Jesus may be even greater.

Yet it all begins with a spiritual seed within us, even as we grew physically from a seed within our mother's womb. When a seed has good ground to grow in, sunlight, and water, it cannot help but grow because all the genetics are in the seed to reproduce after its own kind. That is how we will grow into the likeness of Jesus because His seed is in us and it will reproduce after its own God kind. Our part is to be good fertile ground and to water the seed within us by spending time in God's presence and receiving His Word. Then the seed of God cannot help but grow into the full likeness of Jesus because the seed is already programmed to be like Him. We have this great promise in 1 John 3:2: "Beloved, now we are children of God, and it has not appeared as yet what we shall be. We know that, when He appears, we shall be like Him, because we shall see Him just as He is." For it is by seeing Him that we will be changed into His likeness, going from glory to glory.

Seeing Jesus

These therefore came to Philip, who was from Bethsaida of Galilee, and began to ask him, saying, "Sir, we wish to see Jesus."

John 12:2 (NAS)

Dan Luehrs

What a request: "Sir, we wish to see Jesus." In the mind and heart of God, there could be no greater quest than for people to seek His Son for the right reasons. Were they really searching to know who He was, or were they just wanting to see Him because He was famous? Was it because they wanted to do some name-dropping when telling all their friends they had talked with the man called Jesus of Nazareth, "the miracle worker"? The Bible is very clear about this. These men were not some Jews that were seeking Him, but they were Greeks. Greeks were known for being very religious and intellectuals who had to have it all figured out. I believe they wanted to analyze Jesus and His message so they could figure Him out just like many Christians do today. But Jesus would not meet them as they wanted Him to. He didn't give them a straightforward answer, nor could they figure out the answer that He did give them. In fact, most people reading the following verses today would think Jesus ignored them, not really addressing them:

> And Jesus answered them, saying, "The hour has come for the Son of Man to be glorified." Truly, truly, I say to you, unless a grain of wheat [a seed] falls into the earth and dies, it remains by itself alone; but if it dies, it bears much fruit.
>
> John 12:23–24 (NAS)

Notice the Bible says that Jesus answered them, even though it seems that He did not. But in knowing what we know about the sons of God being manifested in the earth, we can see that He is answering them through wisdom that was far beyond their own understanding. Jesus said that He would be glorified, meaning "to be exulted, honored, and lifted up in heaven and earth." He said in John 17:10 that He is glorified through His people: "And all things that are mine are Thine, and Thine are mine; and I have been glorified in them." What Jesus said to the Greeks and to everybody else there is that if they want to see Him, they are going to have to be looking for Him in a body of believers, even as the grain of wheat falls into the ground and bears much fruit. The fruit or offspring of the seed is what gives glory to the seed. We are the fruit (glory) of that seed which He is speaking of. Jesus Christ is to be glorified in you and me, my friend; we are the fruit of Him. "And the glory which Thou hast given me I have given to them; that they may be one, just as we are one" (John 17:22, NAS). God wants us to be unified as one body in Him, but it can only happen through His glory, not by any human means such as board meetings, committees, or covenants with man. This is a God thing.

The question to be asked is: How do we qualify to become the fruit or seed of Jesus in the earth? The answer is simple, but living it out daily is difficult. Jesus went on to say, "He who loves his life loses it; and he who hates his life in this world shall keep it to life eternal. If anyone serves me, let him follow me; and where I am, there shall my servant also be; if anyone serves me, the Father will honor him" (John 12:25–26, NAS). These verses are God's road map and blueprint, which will bring us to our desired end in Him—His likeness. We must have the desire within us to be like Him so much that we are willing to give up on our dreams and plans in this life. We then will follow Him wherever He goes because we love Him; our greatest need is to be with Him. When a man is in love with his wife, his every thought is to be with her and how he may please her. And so it is with Jesus and His lovely bride. It is His greatest joy to be with her because He delights in her.

God's Offspring

He will see His offspring and prolong His days, and the will of the Lord will prosper in His hand.

Isaiah 53:10 (NIV)

Dan Luehrs

Isaiah 53 is well-known for being the chapter of our suffering Savior who bore our sins and sicknesses upon His own body. Jesus never left any natural children (seed) in the earth to carry His name and it was looked down upon as a curse from God in His day. Isaiah still said, "His offspring would prolong [make long His days in the earth, meaning His seed will continue on]." How could this be? In verse 8, Isaiah asks a question about His seed: "And who can speak of His descendants? For He was cut off from the land of the living; for the transgression of my people He was stricken." Yes, this was another thing that Jesus suffered for us: being stricken and smitten of God, having spiritual children nobody could see but God and Isaiah. How could there be great results from Jesus not having any earthly seed? Because Jesus' seed is spiritual and will never pass away from the earth. In fact, His seed will inherit the earth and all that is in it. One day, every person on earth will know the Lord, from the least to the greatest, and will be born from above. But until that day comes to pass, God has left His seed in the earth to multiply through His sons (seed).

> The field is the world, and the good seed stands for the sons of the kingdom. The weeds are the sons of the evil one.
>
> Matthew 13:38 (NIV)

When a seed of corn is planted in the ground, it will produce more than what was planted. This allows some of the harvest to be eaten and some of the harvest to be used for seed the next planting season. But if a farmer were to eat all of his seed, there would be no crop for next year. God is no fool. He left His seed (us) in the earth when we come into the full likeness of Him. If a seed did not produce after its own kind, there would be no seed to procreate, and I guarantee you that God's seed will reproduce after His kind just as He designed it to. We are the firstfruits of God in the earth, so that means that there will be second fruits, third, etc., after us. "And it was of His own [free] will that He gave us birth [as sons] by [His] Word of Truth, so that we should be a kind of firstfruits of His creatures [a sample of what He created to be consecrated to Himself]" (James 1:18, AMP).

The Chosen Generation

One day while I was reading the genealogy of Jesus in Matthew 1, the Lord spoke to me and said, "You are in this genealogy." At first, I wondered how this could be. Then I realized that I am in it because Jesus lives in me, and that makes me a child of God. We are a *chosen generation* (1 Peter 2:9). We did not choose to follow God; He first called us and saved us by His great power.

> Therefore all the generations from Abraham to David are fourteen generations; and from David to the deportation to Babylon fourteen generations; and from the deportation to Babylon to the time of Christ fourteen generations.
>
> Matthew 1:17 (NAS)

In the first chapter of Matthew, there seems to be a "missing generation." By that, I mean the forty-second generation seems to be missing from this genealogy. Matthew 1:17 says that there are three fourteen generations in the genealogy of Jesus. Yet when you count each name one by one, there are only forty-one, Jesus being the forty-first. So where is the missing forty-second generation? It is found in the sixteenth verse: "And to Jacob was born Joseph the husband of Mary, by whom was born Jesus, who is called Christ." If we count the generations in order, Jesus being the forty-first, then naturally the forty-second one would be the Christ. You might argue that Jesus and the Christ are one in the same. This is true, but you must consider that the word *Christ* is not Jesus' last name, but means "the anointed one" and Jesus

Dan Luehrs

is not the only anointed one. His body is also anointed with the precious oil of the Holy Spirit, as stated in Psalms 133:1–2:

> Behold, how good and how pleasant it is for brothers to dwell together in unity. It is like the precious oil upon the head [Jesus], Coming down upon the beard, even Aaron's beard, coming down upon the edge of his robes [His whole body].

We must understand that Jesus is not alone in His calling to be the Christ. He has a body of believers that are now being conformed into His likeness so that they might do the work of the ministry together in unity. It is the anointing of God that unifies the body of Christ and makes it one: "Now you are Christ's body, and individually members of it" (1 Corinthians 12:27, NAS). Who makes up the Christ? We do.

> For even as the body is one and yet has many members, and all the members of the body, though they are many, are one body, so also is Christ.
>
> 1 Corinthians 12:12 (NAS)

"So also is Christ." Jesus and His body make up the Christ, which is "the anointed one, the overcomer, the deliverer, the Messiah, the Son." "He who overcomes shall inherit these things, and I will be his God and he will be my son" (Revelation 21:7, NAS). The sons of God make up the spiritual offspring of Jesus, the Christ, the forty-second generation, the missing generation, which make up the body of Christ. And this is who we are.

The Mature Man

Today, there are people in heaven that are "the Christ, the mature, the completed man of God" that have been made in the likeness of Jesus. It is not something they could have done for themselves. It was God who worked in them, and it all began with a seed.

> For I am confident of this very thing, that He who began a good work in you will perfect [complete] it until the day of Christ Jesus.
>
> Philippians 1:6 (NAS)

> Faithful is He who calls you [to maturity], and He also will bring it to pass.
>
> 1 Thessalonians 5:24 (NAS)

As we take one day at a time with God and endure to the end, our success is guaranteed because God said He would do it. Even though many people cannot believe God for such great heights in Him, I do because He cannot fail us—if we believe. Again, we are given this great promise in Ephesians 4:13, 15:

> Until we all attain to the unity of the faith, and of the knowledge of the Son of God, to a mature man [body], to the measure of the stature which belongs to the fullness of Christ. But speaking the truth in love, we are to grow up in all aspects into Him, who is the head, even Christ.

Now you may ask, "What does a fully matured son of God look like?" In our natural mind, we might think that he/she would be very successful, popular, and in control of his/her life in every way. After all, that person is perfect. He doesn't have any problems—only joy and peace throughout his life on earth. But if we want to see what a fully matured son really looks like, we just have to look at Jesus. Oh, yes, He had great peace and joy in His life, but He had trials and tribulations that tried Him on every side. In Paul's life, he was going in and out of prisons for the sake

Dan Luehrs

of the gospel, and his many beatings made him like Jesus. While we would like to have what he has today in heaven and throughout eternity, are we willing to allow God to conform us into His likeness through any fashion that He prescribes in our life? If you want to be like Jesus, I can guarantee you that your life will not be what you would have wanted or would have chosen. God does know what is best for us. There is one primary thing that God is trying to work in us: His love. There is no other word that fully explains what God is and what He wants us to become, for it is the length, the breath, the height, and depth of God. And He wants us to be filled up with it.

> So that Christ may dwell in your hearts through faith; and that you, being rooted and grounded in love, may be able to comprehend with all the saints what is the breadth and length and height and depth, and to know the love of Christ which surpasses knowledge, that you may be filled up to all the fullness of God.
>
> Ephesians 3:17–19 (NAS)

Your Name Written Down in Glory

All I have written so far is to prepare you for what I am about to show you. If you cannot receive or believe that God has such a high calling and destiny for you, you will not be able to conceive that He has much, much more for you than you could ever imagine. The book of Revelation gives us more than just a glimpse into the future of God's chosen ones. It proclaims it loudly and clearly for those who have ears to hear what the Holy Spirit is saying to the church. Please read the following verses carefully, realizing that John is not writing about a physical city but about a people who have been prepared to be the wife and bride of Jesus, for they have become like Him:

And one of the seven angels who had the seven bowls full of the seven last plagues, came and spoke with me, saying, "Come here, I shall show you the bride, the wife of the Lamb." And he carried me away in the Spirit to a great and high mountain, and showed me the holy city, Jerusalem, coming down out of heaven from God [the bride], having the glory of God. Her brilliance was like a very costly stone, as a stone of crystal-clear jasper.

Revelation 21:9–11 (NAS)

Notice how the glory of God radiates from her because God has made her like Himself as crystal-clear jasper stone. Revelation 4:3 says, "And He who was sitting [on the throne] was like a jasper stone and a sardius in appearance; and there was a rainbow around the throne, like an emerald in appearance." Even as God is, so shall we be. What a marvelous promise God has given to us.

It [the bride] had a great and high wall, with twelve gates, and at the gates twelve angels; and names were written on them, which are the twelve tribes of Israel. There were three gates on the east and three gates on the north and three gates on the south and three gates on the west. And the wall of the city had twelve foundation stones, and on them were the twelve names of the twelve apostles of the Lamb.

Revelation 21:12–14 (NAS)

One day while reading these verses, I understood the great honor God had bestowed upon the twelve tribes of Israel and the twelve apostles by eternally memorializing their names in the city of God (who we are). Remember that this is, not a literal city, but a people made into the likeness of Jesus. "Having been built upon the foundation of the apostles and prophets, Christ Jesus Himself being the corner stone" (Ephesians 2:20, NAS). The foundation is set within us through the lives and teachings of the apostles that

Dan Luehrs

we are building upon—truth upon truth. We must not stay on the level of the foundation but keep going higher into the things of God, to be changed into His likeness through our tribulations.

Notice what verse 12 said: "It [the bride] had a great and high wall." These people had gone higher in the things of God, having built upon the foundational truths that were given to them. It's not that we are any greater than they were, but that we have grown in truth and numbers, as spiritual stones that make up the city of God. For that's what a city is—people (1 Peter 2:5, NAS). Each one of us is building something in our spirit man whether we know it or not. Either we are becoming more like Jesus in our spirit, or we are not. It all has to do with the building materials we are using, such as the religious and world system, which are wood, hay, and straw. These building materials are not long-lasting but will burn up. But if we build our lives with the Spirit of truth, we will be building with gold, silver, precious stones, which are only purified by fire: "Now if any man builds upon the foundation with gold, silver, precious stones, wood, hay, straw" (1 Corinthians 3:12, NAS). Notice that it says, "If any man builds." We are the "any man" that is now building his life upon something that is lasting *or* something that will burn up in our trials. We must thank God for our trials by fire because they are causing us to become more like Him.

> Each man's work will become evident; for the day will show it, because it is to be revealed with fire; and the fire itself will test the quality of each man's work. If any man's work which he has built upon it remains, he shall receive a reward. If any man's work is burned up, he shall suffer loss; but he himself shall be saved, yet so as through fire. Do you not know that you are a temple of God, and that the Spirit of God dwells in you? If any man destroys the temple of God, God will destroy him, for the temple of God is holy, and that is what you are.
>
> 1 Corinthians 3:13–17 (NAS)

Do we not understand that we are now building God's temple within ourselves by what we are partaking of and by living it out each day in the fires of our life? We are. A person is what they eat in the natural and what they partake of in the spirit realm. If we are partaking of the things of God, which is present truth, we are building correctly upon the foundation. However, when people begin to suffer and go through fires, they often stop going forward with the building process in their lives, not realizing that these fires are now proving the quality of their work and showing what their life is built upon. Is the truth of God really in our heart, or is it only in our head? "Each man's work will become evident; for the day will show it, because it is to be revealed with fire" (1 Corinthians 3:13, NASV). The day of testing is the day that Paul is writing about and not the day we die. We must realize that when we pass the test by going through the fire, God will reward us with a greater revelation of Himself. Then we can be changed into His likeness. There is no greater reward in life than to have the revelation of Jesus Christ within our hearts and then one day unveil Him to a hurting world.

It is through the gates of suffering and tribulation that we enter into the kingdom.

> And the twelve gates were twelve pearls; each one of the gates was a single pearl...
>
> Revelation 21:21

Huge pearls are the gateway into the city of God. I know that tradition has taught us that these are natural pearls. But what are pearls in the natural? They are small stones caused by irritants that have become beautiful gemstones in the oyster's mouth. It has overcome these grains of sand and turned them into precious stones by having to deal with them on a daily basis. Our daily tribulations (stones) that we have overcome will be the pearly gates that lead us into the city of God. We must not run from our trials any longer but embrace them instead so they will become the pearly gates to the kingdom of God for us. Paul said in Acts 14:22, "Through many tribulations we must enter the kingdom of God." The only way for us to enter into the fullness of God is for us to go through great tribulations that He allows in our life. And we must thank Him for them because there is no other way for us to enter into the fullness of the kingdom of God.

As the Lord began to show me this great honor He has bestowed upon the twelve tribes and apostles, He also showed me that we are also named in this great city of God, even as we are named among the genealogy of Jesus.

> He who overcomes, I will make him a pillar in the temple of my God, and he will not go out from it anymore; and I will write upon him the name of my God, and the name of the city of my God, the new Jerusalem [who we are], which comes down out of heaven from my God, and my new name.
>
> Revelation 3:12 (NAS)

Remember that we the body and bride of Jesus make up the city. Now let me show you how we are named and remembered in the city.

> And he who talked with me had a gold reed to measure the city, its gates, and its wall. The city is laid out as a square; its length is as great as its breadth. And he measured the city with the reed: twelve thousand furlongs. Its length, breadth, and height are equal.
>
> Revelation 21:15–16 (NKJV)

Now remember that Paul prayed for us that we would "be able to comprehend with all the saints what is the breadth and length and height and depth" (Ephesians 3:18). God wants us to know these truths, and in the book of Revelation, it is given to us. It is interesting to note that in Revelation 11, John was given a measuring reed to measure the temple (that we are), but he was told not to measure the outer court. In other words, it was not yet complete, so don't spend your time there. But now in chapter 21, he is told to measure the whole city and to know that its length, breadth, and height are equal. The people who make up this city are now equal and are made complete in it; they are the finished product as prophesied Revelation 10:7: "But in the days of the voice of the seventh angel, when he is about to sound, then the mystery of God is finished, as He preached to His servants the prophets." They are now a finished temple and have been perfected by Him because they have come into the full likeness of Jesus. Remember, Paul wrote in Ephesians 4:13, 15:

> Until we all attain to the unity of the faith, and of the knowledge of the Son of God, to a mature man [body], to the measure of the stature, which belongs to the fullness of Christ. But speaking the truth in love, we are to grow up in all aspects into Him, who is the head, even Christ.

These people are the body of Christ who have grown in love and are made equal on all sides with no one person greater than the other. To be equal means "identical in size; quantity; value; having the same privileges, rights, status, and opportunities as others; and being evenly balanced between opposing sides." The Scriptures are very clear that we are joint-heirs with Jesus. This means that one will not do something without the other; they are equals (Romans 8:17, NKJV). When this unification takes place, the body of Christ will have fulfilled the Lord's priestly prayer:

> And the glory which Thou hast given me I have given to them; that they may be one, just as we are one; I in them, and Thou in me, that they may be perfected [complete] in unity, that the world may know that Thou

didst send me, and didst love them, even as Thou didst love me.

John 17:22–23 (NAS)

When this takes place in its completeness, the body will have become one like the Godhead. Notice that the world, not the church, will stand up and take notice that God did send Jesus for them. It is through the sons of God ministry that the world will come to know Jesus.

Named in the One Hundred Forty-Four

Then he measured its wall: one hundred and forty-four cubits, according to the measure of a man, that is, of an angel.

Revelation 21:17 (NKJV)

As I read this next verse in Revelation 21 telling how the wall measured 144 cubits, I realized that twelve times twelve equals one hundred forty-four. What makes that significant is that there are twelve tribes and twelve apostles; the culmination of their numbers is one hundred forty-four. Twelve is the number of God's government, and that is what the body of Christ is: the ruling, governing body throughout the earth. We must understand that the numbered 144,000 people of the tribes of Israel is a symbolic number. It is, not a literal number, but represents something much greater than just a few people—the whole body of Christ throughout the ages. I have asked God about the 144,000 for years and still wasn't able to get a clear revelation on it until I saw this verse. I knew then that my answer was here.

The word *according* is not in the Greek but was added by the translator. We read on: "Then he measured its wall [who we are]: one hundred and forty-four cubits, the measure of the man [the fullness of Christ], which is, the messenger of God." Simply put, you and I are numbered in the symbolic 144,000 messengers if we go on to know the Lord, growing into the full likeness of Him. Again, remember that Paul called the body of Christ the mature or perfected man. "A mature [complete] man, to the measure of the stature which belongs to the fullness of Christ" (Ephesians 4:13, NAS).

In Revelation 14:1, we see the 144,000 standing on Mount Zion with Jesus because they have been made complete in Him. Mount Zion is symbolic of the government or throne of God, even as Mount Zion was the government and throne of King David in history. "And I looked, and behold, the Lamb was standing on Mount Zion, and with Him one hundred and forty-four thousand, having His name and the name [the character] of His Father written on their foreheads" (Revelation 14:1, NAS).

We first read of the 144,000 in Revelation 7 when the tribes are marked with the seal of God. Their minds have been sealed with their Father's name as they appear on Mount Zion and are changed through their trials and tribulations of climbing to the top. Each one of these tribes named in Revelation 7:5–8 is an attribute of the Christian faith. We must remember that many of the Old Testament characters and stories are types and shadows to give the New Testament spiritual understanding. We must be careful with our interpretation of the book of Revelation because much of it is symbolic.

Their names and meanings are:

- Judah: "Praise"

    "I will bless the LORD at all times; His praise shall continually be in my mouth" (Psalms 34:1).

- Reuben: "See a son"

    The overcoming Church is God's son. "He who overcomes shall inherit these things, and I will be his God and he will be my son" (Revelation 21:7).

Dan Luehrs

- Gad: "To overcome"

  "He who overcomes shall inherit these things, and I will be his God and he will be my son" (Revelation 21:7).

- Asher: "Happy"

  "Then on the twenty-third day of the seventh month he sent the people to their tents, rejoicing and happy of heart because of the goodness that the LORD had shown to David and to Solomon and to His people Israel" (2 Chronicles 7:10).

- Naphtali: "Wrestling"

  "For we wrestle not against flesh and blood, but against principalities, against powers, against the rulers of the darkness of this world, against spiritual wickedness in high places" (Ephesians 6:12, KJV).

- Manasseh: "God causes me to forget all my sufferings."

  "And Joseph named the first-born Manasseh, For he said, 'God has made me forget all my trouble and all my father's household'" (Genesis 41:51).

- Simeon: "Hearing"

  "My sheep hear my voice, and I know them, and they follow me" (John 10:27).

- Levi: "Unity"

  "Behold, how good and how pleasant it is for brothers to dwell together in unity" (Psalms 133:1).

- Issachar: "Reward"

  "After these things the word of the LORD came unto Abram in a vision, saying, 'Fear not, Abram: I am thy shield, and thy exceeding great reward'" (Genesis 15:1, KJV).

- Zebulun: "Habitation"

  We are the dwelling place of God.

"In whom ye also are builded together for an habitation of God through the Spirit" (Ephesians 2:22, KJV).

- Joseph: "Add a son"

  Jesus is the firstborn Son, and we are added in with Him.

  "And she called his name Joseph; and said, The LORD shall add to me another son" (Genesis 30:24, KJV).

- Benjamin: "Son of my right hand"

  We will be at the right hand of the Father with Jesus.

  "And it came to pass, as her soul was in departing [for she died], that she called his name Benoni: but his father called him Benjamin" (Genesis 35:18, KJV).

Yes, each one of us is to have these characteristics as an overcoming Christian if we want to be sealed with His name. Why and how are they sealed, or in another term, "marked" for God? God has *His* people marked for Himself, and Satan has people marked for *him*.

Conclusion

As Christians, we are to be the good seed God is planting in the lives of other people. But what will we grow up to be, you may ask? Trees of life that produces fruit, which other people may eat. Throughout the Bible, there are verses that speak of this very thing.

> And he shall be like a tree planted by the rivers of water, that bringeth forth his fruit in his season; his leaf also shall not wither; and whatsoever he doeth shall prosper.
>
> Psalms 1:3 (NAS)

> For he will be like a tree planted by the water, that extends its roots by a stream and will not fear when the

heat comes; but its leaves will be green, and it will not be anxious in a year of drought nor cease to yield fruit.

Jeremiah 17:8 (NAS)

That they might be called trees of righteousness, the planting of the LORD, that he might be glorified.

Isaiah 61:3 (KJV)

Just as there are many types and shadows in the Bible about what the Holy Spirit is like—wind, rain, wine—there are different types and shadows of what the body of Christ is known as a body, a bride, a son, an overcomer, a cloud, and trees. Again, most people cannot fathom that we become a tree of life just like Jesus. People might say that Jesus is the only tree of life and that it could not include us because we are but mere worms and worthy of nothing. It is true that we are nothing and are not worthy of anything, but because of God's goodness and love, He has called us to be the bearers of His life and love.

Please read this next verse carefully.

And he showed me a river of the water of life, clear as crystal, coming from the throne of God and of the Lamb, in the middle of its street. And on either side of the river was the tree of life, bearing twelve kinds of fruit, yielding its fruit every month; and the leaves of the tree were for the healing of the nations.

Revelation 22:1–2 (NAS)

Notice that there is more than just one tree, but there are many trees lining the middle of the street and on both sides of the river. The fruit and seed of the original tree of life is Jesus and He has reproduced many trees in His own likeness. Hallelujah! Notice that the trees are producing fruit each month, and fruit has seed in it. This tells me that one day the sons of God are going to teach the nations the great truths of the Bible, so they will believe the truth rather than the lies of man and Satan. The very leaves of the trees are for the restoration of the nations. We can see clearly that God does, not intend for mankind to be destroyed by His wrath, but restored through the ministry of His sons so that humanity is fully restored back to God.

May God bless you richly as you ponder these wonderful truths in His Word, and may God bring His revelation of them to you.

Dan Luehrs

Grace, God's Indescribable Gift

Thanks be to God for His indescribable gift.

2 Corinthians 9:15, NAS

This message on the grace of God I consider to be one of the greatest revelation, I have ever received from the Lord, for it has taken me some twenty-five years to see that *grace* is probably the second greatest word and gift in all of the Bible behind *love*. What I share with you has come through much of these twenty-five years of suffering the will of God for my life. Oh, what lies many preachers have spoken to the church of not having to suffer in God's will, for they have stolen from the church some of the greatest truths and riches from the people of God. And that truth is grace in the time of tribulation. I can only pray that you will also get a glimpse of His glory in this one marvelous word.

The first time I noticed God's grace in my life was in the late 1980s when I started preaching. My church was going through some pastoral changes, and I was asked to preach twice on Sundays in the morning and evening services. I was still working a full-time job, and I asked the Lord how I could have time to prepare two messages for the people. He just gave me peace that He was well able to give me what the people needed.

At that time, I did not understand that messages from the Lord are not studied up out of the Bible through my mind, but they were downloaded from heaven into my spirit man and then unpacked by the Lord for the people to hear. As the Lord was doing this through me, I could feel His grace upon me. This was my first lesson in grace, and it was marvelous, easy, and exciting. When God's grace is upon you to do something, it will not be complicated or difficult because the oil of the Holy Spirit will make it all come together with His joy and peace. But when we have to sweat at it, is when we are doing things in our own power and strength.

The second time I found grace working in my heart was when I became senior pastor of a church that had been there for fifty years, and many of the people had been there most of that time. In this church, I spoke three times a week, and I felt over-whelmed at coming up with something fresh each week to give to these people. Many of them were well seasoned in the Lord and His Word, so how could I being so young and ever hope to feed them fresh manna each time.

One day, I knelt down before the Lord and said, "Lord, I think I have bit off more than I can chew."

All God said was, "Just trust me."

I said okay. He never had missed a message for all those years I was there. To show that God did this through me, one elderly lady that had been in the church from the beginning said to me when I was leaving the church, "You are one of the finest preachers that

Dan Luehrs

I have ever sat under." That floored me because I knew it was, not I she was speaking of, but the Lord working through me.

The next time that I felt grace working in me was to stay in His will when I wanted to quit and run. I felt Him upon me to persevere every day even though life made no sense whatsoever. My first wife was opposed to me being in the ministry, and she made it known to me that she did not want anything to do with me and my ministry. At that time, the Lord was telling me to write all the things that He had given me. It took two years and six books later before I was done with the task; the grace of God was on me to complete it. Writing was my full-time job, and somehow, the Lord paid all the bills through that time. When I was done writing, all the bills were paid. My former wife would look at me in my office and would say, "Don't you go nuts sitting in here?" I would look around the room and sense God everywhere, and I would say no. When I look back and see how God gave me His grace to live with her badgering me because I was, not bringing a weekly check, but just trusting God to bring in the money, it was truly grace that brought me through. Little did I know that time was just preparation for the next test God had in my life and how much I would have to lean upon His grace because I had no strength left within me to go on. This is where my story of understanding grace more starts.

One night, I was given a continuous vision of a cup being formed on a wood lathe. The lathe was spinning the piece of wood as it was being formed into a cup. I saw this for a very long time from many different angles and became somewhat tired of seeing it because I wanted to go to bed. It was not until a few days later that I understood what the Lord was saying to me. God made my cup just for me; the cup is the circumstances of my life right now that I was to drink of. The next day, I went in to my office, and there was a wooden cup there like the one I had just seen in my vision the night before. My wife must have put it there without knowing that I had my vision, but I took it as a sure sign that God had spoken to me. Even though I cannot go into the specifics of what was going on in my life, I can tell you that it was the most ongoing trial that I had ever faced with no seeming way out. Even though going through financial pressure is most difficult, this was even more trying because my flesh wanted to quit, but God says, "Don't give up." When God says don't give up, He wants to teach us something of lasting value through the trial.

A sign that things were about to change for my good happened as I parked my car, and I looked at the mileage counter, which I almost never do, and it said, "555-1." Then I caught a glimpse of the speedometer, and it said "555-1." Then I came into the house and caught the closing moments on a TV show, and it said "Grace Films." In biblical numerology, *five* is the number of grace. I did need great grace to see me through this time because I had been so accustomed to it before since I was always seemingly going through something that required the grace of God on me. But for many months, I did not have it, and I missed it and did not understand that to require grace, one must have need of it. God will not give it to us unless we are in need of it, then we will not take it for granted. Now I realize to have the manifested grace required me to go through times of tribulation so that God would give me this wonderful gift. I believe what God is saying to me through the "555" is that He is going to give me His triple grace to get through this difficult time.

At this time, Jesus appeared to me in a church service, and He grabbed my two hands and pulled me up twice and said, "Come with me." I believe what He was saying to me was to come up in the spirit realm with Him and stay there and receive my life and grace from Him, for that's what grace really is: His life. One week later, God's presence came on me in great power that gave me so much strength that I felt like a new man with a new life. I received a prophetic word shortly after this, and the Lord said, "How could it be any other way, but the way of my cross? What did you think that the way would be paved with gold to My glory? It is always the way of the cross. Quit looking at the needs of your flesh and what you are lacking and come on the segue of the cross to My glory. For I have set up your life experiences so you could die to self. You cannot give up, for if you keep going, you will win." The cross of Christ is always with us if we are one of His elect, for there is no other way to enter the kingdom of God. If we are living the crucified life, we know that we are on the true path of life that will lead us to the fullness of God.

I have been living in a garment of God's presence around the clock. When I find myself slipping back into self-pity, I begin to fellowship with God, and I am right there where I was before in the spirit realm with Him to get my strength and peace back. What a wonderful way to live—the way God design man to live in His presence, but it seems to come with a great price that many people are not willing to pay because it is costly for them to give up earthly comforts.

More than Enough

Peter, an apostle of Jesus Christ, to the pilgrims of the Dispersion in Pontus, Galatia, Cappadocia, Asia, and Bithynia, elect according to the foreknowledge of God the Father, in sanctification of the Spirit, for obedience and sprinkling of the blood of Jesus Christ: Grace to you and peace be multiplied.

1 Peter 1:1–2 (NKJV)

Peter addressed his letter to the pilgrims of the dispersion. Who were the pilgrims of that day, and what was the dispersion of that day? The pilgrims were Christians that were on the run for their lives because of their faith in Jesus Christ and were being scattered through all the known earth. Many hid in caves and in the wilderness to stay alive and were hunted down as wild animals so that their faith would not be spread to others. In other words, Satan was dogging their tracks with great intensity, but Peter was given a word by God to not give in but to receive God's grace in the midst of their trial. This is why he tells them to think it not strange.

> How blessed is the man whose strength [grace] is in Thee; in whose heart are the highways to Zion. Passing through the valley of Baca [weeping], they make it a spring, the early rain also covers it with blessings. They go from strength [grace] to strength (grace), every one of them appears before God in Zion.
>
> Psalms 84:5–7 (NAS)

> May grace and peace be yours in fullest measure.
>
> 1 Peter 1:2 (NAS)

What greater blessing could Peter have bestowed upon us than the grace and peace of God? Grace and peace work hand in hand, the two are traveling buddies; in my opinion, peace works within me as does grace, but somehow God gives us this strength within to be worked out through the weakness of our flesh. God's grace is His strength or power to get through anything that we may face in life. No devil, no demon, or principality will stop the grace of God because it is the power of God. There is no greater force in all of creation.

> And He said to me, "My grace is sufficient for you, for my strength is made perfect in weakness." Therefore most gladly I will rather boast in my infirmities, that the power of Christ may rest upon me.
>
> 2 Corinthians 12:9 (NKJV)

For years I have wondered at this verse like a dog that cocks his head when his master is talking to him, and the dog looks at him

Dan Luehrs

with wonderment of what he had just said. So it was with this verse, but today, I can say that God has allowed me to see a little deeper into grace than ever before. I am convinced that most people do not have a clue of what Paul was saying here, for it is only with head knowledge that most people see it, as it was with me; it is only going through trials that we can ever come to know of it. I maybe off the deep-end here, but somehow I believe that grace is a spirit being that God sends upon our physical flesh to strengthen us so that we can feel Him in a tangible way. Why else did Paul say, "That the power of Christ may rest upon me"? Paul felt the reality of the presence of God *upon* himself.

Before grace came upon me, I had two angelic visitations very close together. I think they were just preparing me for what was to come. All I know is that God has given me many confirmations that this is His will for my life to be here in this place until He is done with me. If I were to leave my trial, I would be going in the power of my flesh, which would be much scarier for me than to stay put, patiently waiting for God to change me into what He would have me to be, even though my flesh is very weak. I have found that if I run from one trial, I just run into another one that is worse than the one I had before. I think the old saying goes, "From the pan into the fire." Even though the pan is hot, the fire is far worse, so stay in the pan.

Paul would rather boast of his weakness in the flesh, not his strengths. Our generation is prone to boast in themselves because we really don't know God's power in our weaknesses as we should; plus, we want to feel good about ourselves when there is no good thing within us. When we become transparent, we are humbling ourselves before others and before the Lord, and He can only bless this because God gives His grace or power to the humble. "But He gives a greater grace. Therefore it says, 'God is opposed to the proud, but gives grace to the humble'" (James 4:6, NAS). To most the garment of humility is very ugly and embarrassing because it is lowly and un-esteemed to the flesh, and few want it because they have to go too low in following the Lord to get it.

If you are in a dead-end job or are married to the most horrible person in the world and feel like you are nothing, but somehow you still feel like you are in the will of God, rejoice in it because God will bestow upon you His most indescribable gift of grace if you will just continue to be thankful in all things rather than feeling sorry for yourself.

God told Paul that His grace was sufficient or that it was enough for Paul to get through his time of testing. One of God's names is El-Shaddai: "The God that is more than enough." When we have God's grace, we have Him. I have no other words than to describe it to you this way. Yes, we have God with us at all times whether we feel Him or not, but what I am talking about is the manifest power of God that is with you twenty-four-seven. His presence will keep you strong and from giving into the tribulation that you may be facing at that time in your life. If you do not need grace, you will not get it; but when you cry out to God for strength, you will receive it. This is why Paul could say, "Therefore I take pleasure in infirmities, in reproaches, in needs, in persecutions, in distresses, for Christ's sake. For when I am weak, then I am strong" (2 Corinthians 12:10, NKJV).

How in the world could Paul take pleasure in tribulation? Was he a nut, did he like pain that much? No, Paul was so in love with the presence of God that it was worth everything to him. God was so great on him and in him that the trial seemed as nothing to the greatness of God's presence. To put it plainly: Paul's spirit was abiding in heavenly places with Jesus while his flesh was undergoing great pressures from the world, the flesh, and the devil. In fact, Paul said in Romans 8:18, "For I consider that the sufferings of this present time are not worthy to be compared with the glory that is to be revealed to us." To think and talk like this is truly supernatural because the natural man just wants to complain about his problems. But according to Paul and the Word of God, we can rejoice by faith in tribulation as His grace comes upon us; we can rejoice with joy unspeakable and full of glory. Hallelujah!

Dan Luehrs

Grace in Tribulation

> Now, brethren, we wish to make known to you the
> grace of God which has been given in the churches
> of Macedonia: that in a great ordeal of affliction their
> abundance of joy and their deep poverty overflowed in
> the wealth of their liberality.
>
> 2 Corinthians 8:1–2 (NAS)

Paul clearly wants to teach the church about grace: "We wish to
make known to you the grace of God." Most people in the ministry interpret 2 Corinthians chapters 8 and 9 about the giving of
money, but I see something much greater than money that God
wants to give to His people, and that is grace. God wants to give
us this in our time of need so that we can give it to others.

> Blessed be the God and Father of our Lord Jesus Christ,
> the Father of mercies and God of all comfort; who com-
> forts us in all our affliction so that we may be able to
> comfort those who are in any affliction with the com-
> fort with which we ourselves are comforted by God.
>
> 2 Corinthians 1:3–4 (NAS)

There is no greater comfort in the entire world than God's grace
in the time of need.

Paul starts his discourse on grace in chapter 8, and he finishes
it with chapter 9 verses fourteen and fifteen: "While they also,
by prayer on your behalf, yearn for you because of the surpass-
ing grace of God in you. Thanks be to God for His indescribable gift [grace]." Grace is the gift that God wants His people to
receive so that they can make it through their tribulations with
His power to overcome and not to fail. God wants you to lean
and rely upon Him heavily because you do not have the strength

within yourself to make it through to the end. God has an end-less supply of grace to give you daily if you will just seek Him for it. Ask, seek, and you will receive. In order to get through the days that are ahead of us in our own private lives and with the earth reeling with birth pains one after another, we are going to have to learn how to live by the grace of God. Even as the first-century church learned grace through great trial, so must we.

> So we urged Titus, that as he had begun, so he would also complete this grace in you as well. But as you abound in everything—in faith, in speech, in knowl-edge, in all diligence, and in your love for us—see that you abound in this grace also.
>
> 2 Corinthians 8:6–7 (NKJV)

God, not only wants us to have grace, but to abound in it. That means to be filled with *all* the fullness of His grace. "May grace and peace be yours in fullest measure" (1 Peter 1:2, NAS). Wow, what a God we serve that fills us with everything that we need to make it to our journey's end. "And God is able to make all grace abound to you, that always having all sufficiency [contentment] in everything, you may have an abundance [of grace] for every good deed" (2 Corinthians 9:8, NAS). Would you not want to have all God's grace? Of course you would. Then ask Him for it right now and see what God does with you. Don't get discouraged if nothing happens right away but wait and see what God will do for you because He has many avenues that He can take to help you. You never know when or how He will show up strong on your behalf.

> For you know the grace of our Lord Jesus Christ, that though He was rich, yet for your sake He became poor, that you through His poverty might become rich [in grace].
>
> 2 Corinthians 8:9 (NAS)

Dan Luehrs

Paul wants us to understand that if Jesus needed grace to get through this earthly existence, certainly we will also need it. Jesus came from the glory of the Father into a hellish atmosphere of demonic oppression even as we live in it daily. But most likely, He had much more demonic powers coming against Him then because the enemy knew who He was and tried to cause Him to fall over and over. I'm sure when Jesus was a child or in His youth, the demons could not understand how He could not sin as other children did because the fullness of grace was upon Him. As I was led by the Holy Spirit to read these verses in the Gospel of John, I shouted because I see them in a new light of grace as never before and understand that Jesus is grace in our life, for He is all that we will ever need. Grace upon grace is given to us whenever we receive it from Him.

> And the Word became flesh and dwelt among us, and we beheld His glory, the glory as of the only begotten of the Father, full of grace and truth. John bore witness of Him and cried out, saying, "This was He of whom I said, 'He who comes after me is preferred before me, for He was before me.'" And of His fullness we have all received, and grace for grace. For the law was given through Moses, but grace and truth came through Jesus Christ.
>
> John 1:14–17 (NKJV)

Jesus just did not have grace; He was full of grace because He is grace. And it is through Him that we have grace upon grace overflowing in our life. Oh, what a wonderful Savior we have. He is in us, around us, and before us. So why do we have to fear anything whatsoever in this life if God is everywhere and He is going to give us all things that pertain to life and godliness throughout our life on planet earth?

The Grace That Has Come

May grace and peace be yours in fullest measure.

1 Peter 1:2 (NAS)

Grace and peace be multiplied to you in the knowledge
of God and of Jesus our Lord.

2 Peter 1:2 (NAS)

In the books that bear Peter's name, he encourages the people of
God to receive the fullness of grace in our quest to know Christ
more so that we may be changed into His likeness. In fact, we
will not come to know Him more unless we do receive His grace
because grace is a revelation of Jesus to us. So why not seek all
the grace that is available to us? But I warn you that the greater
grace is given only because we are going through something that
requires it. Peter begins the first chapter of 1 Peter with the fullness of grace to come upon us at the coming of the Lord Jesus
Christ: "Therefore, gird your minds for action, keep sober in
spirit, fix your hope completely on the grace to be brought to
you at the revelation of Jesus Christ" (1 Peter 1:13, NAS). How
do we fix our hope completely on grace? Remember that Jesus
is grace and that grace is the strength of God to get us through
something, which is for us to possess the full likeness of Jesus.
Think of grace as a painkiller of sorts so that God can do whatever internal surgery on us because without it, we just simply will
not make it through. The revelation of Jesus is the appearing of
the Christ within His saints because we cannot prepare ourselves
for this great event, so God gives us grace that will assist us and
carry us through to the finished work. We must set our hope
completely on the grace of God to do this in us, for there is no
other thing for us to look to but God's grace, whether it comes
by His Word, the Holy Spirit, enemy, or friend. God has many
avenues and is never at loss of what He can do or use in making
us like His Son. Oh, how God loves us.

Dan Luehrs

Peter ends his first book exhorting us to continue in the grace of God; in fact, he says, "Stand firm in it." This is a command for us not to rely upon anything but grace (God's strength). "Through Silvanus, our faithful brother [for so I regard him], I have written to you briefly, exhorting and testifying that this is the true grace of God. Stand firm in it" (1 Peter 5:12, NAS). I have heard many things about the books of Peter, but I have never heard anyone say that Peter was writing about grace. Some people think that maybe Peter was a little too harsh in his writing and that he might have copied some from the book of Jude because of their likeness. With a little study, we can see that Peter is writing about grace and is trying to prepare us for the Lord's coming because this is his theme throughout his writings so that we can come to the desired end that God would have for us.

"As to this salvation, the prophets who prophesied of the grace that would come to you made careful search and inquiry" (1 Peter 1:10, NAS). I believe we are living in the time that the prophets foresaw grace coming upon God's people to prepare them for the coming of the Lord. Yes, great grace will be given to us when the Lord comes, but I am more focused on the grace that I need right now to make it through this trial that I am facing. I want to pass this test so that I am ready for the next one, which will require more faith and more grace to get me through. Then I can agree with Paul: "I take pleasure in my weakness so that the power of Christ may be upon me." What better way to live then by the power of God. For we have this promise: "And after you have suffered for a little while, the God of all grace, who called you to His eternal glory in Christ, will Himself perfect, confirm, strengthen and establish you [in Christ's likeness]" (1 Peter 5:10, NAS). Do you see that it is God's will for us to suffer so that He can complete us and make us like His Son? Unless we can see the glory that comes from our suffering, we will not be able to walk in all the spiritual authority that God would have us to. So many Christians think that because Jesus suffered, we don't have to; but they fail to realize that God is not asking us to suffer on the cross for our sins, but that we enter into the sufferings of Christ that make us one with Him and sets us on the throne with Him. It was through suffering that He was able to sit upon His throne, and it is only through suffering that we will be able to also.

> Who are protected by the power of God [grace] through faith for a salvation ready to be revealed in the last time.
>
> 1 Peter 1:5 (NAS)

If we are protected by the power of God, what do we have to fear anyway if all things are working out for the glory of God in our life? Our suffering will cause us to grow in God's grace because we will have to learn to lean on Him just a little more each time. "But grow in the grace and knowledge of our Lord and Savior Jesus Christ. To Him be the glory, both now and to the day of eternity. Amen" (2 Peter 3:18, NAS). We are to be growing in grace, but how would we ever grow if we never had any trials in life to prove that we have a need for it or even what it is? For His grace is made perfect in weakness, and if we want His grace, which is also His presence, we will need to go through some things in life to require God's assistance upon us.

How do we know if we are growing in grace? When we are weak, then we are strong for His strength, and joy will be upon us in our time of the trial, which can only come from one source—God. Remember this one simple fact: joy in tribulation is from God, and depression is from the devil. That's why the Scriptures say, "Rejoice always; pray without ceasing; in everything give thanks; for this is God's will for you in Christ Jesus" (1 Thessalonians 5:16–18, NAS). Rejoicing in trials can only come from God because the natural man wants to sulk, but our spirit man wants to rejoice in it because he knows that God is working in the tribulation for our benefit in the end. Remember these words from Winston Churchill when Germany wanted England to surrender, "Never give up, never, never, never."

Dan Luehrs

Let There Be Light in You

In the beginning God created the heavens and the earth. The earth was without form, and void; and darkness was on the face of the deep. And the Spirit of God was hovering over the face of the waters. Then God said, "Let there be light"; and there was light. And God saw the light, that it was good; and God divided the light from the darkness. God called the light Day, and the darkness He called Night. So the evening and the morning were the first day.

Genesis 1:1–5 (NKJV)

We are living in a time when deep darkness is on the face of the earth again as it was in the beginning of creation. So where does the darkness come from, both now and before the day of creation? Did God create the world in darkness? No, the Bible declares in 1 John 1:5, "That God is light and in Him is no darkness at all." The book of Genesis states that everything that God created in the beginning "was good," but when He made man, He said, "It was very good" (verse 31). Man was created in the light of God, so we know that God did not create the darkness found in him after the fall. So why is there such darkness on the earth both now and then if God did not create it? One word: sin.

The darkness that is over the earth at this time and in the beginning came from sin; we know from Scripture that Satan and his fallen angels are beings of darkness, and they have no light in them: "For we do not wrestle against flesh and blood, but against principalities, against powers, against the rulers of the darkness of this age, against spiritual hosts of wickedness in the heavenly places" (Ephesians 6:12, NKJV). We must understand that the rulers of darkness want to bring their depravity into our souls, even as they live in the darkness themselves. Biblical darkness means to be living absent of the knowledge and truth of Jesus Christ. In other words, if we are living a life of willful sin with no regret and repentance of our sin, we are living in darkness, which is opposite of living a life of light and truth.

Satan, who we believe to have been named Lucifer, means "the morning star or the light-bringer" in Hebrew. He was a light-giving being at one time before he fell into sin and became the epitome of all darkness and sin. In fact, the Bible says that there are other fallen angels held in chains of darkness unto this day because at one time they obviously sinned against God: "For if God did not spare the angels who sinned, but cast them down to hell and delivered them into chains of darkness, to be reserved for judgment" (2 Peter 2:4, NKJV). So we know without a doubt that powerful angelic beings were once walking in the light and knowledge of God and fell away from Him by disobeying His law. The question I have is: why did God not forgive them as He has done for us? My guess is that they could see God in their own

Dan Luehrs

realm, as we cannot, and they did not have to live by faith like we must; so in a way, faith protects us.

When the devil deceived Eve and caused her to sin against God, he already had darkness within himself to have been able to infect her and us with it. "For you were once darkness, but now you are light in the Lord. Walk as children of light" (Ephesians 5:8–9, NKJV). We must understand that we were once as dark as Satan himself, full of sin and death with no hope of ever being in the light of God. But now, Jesus, the light of the world, has come into our hearts giving us the knowledge and light that God is. But before we can understand why we need the light, we must know why the light had to come to us in the first place.

The Darkness

How have you fallen from heaven, O light-bringer and daystar, son of the morning. How you have been cut down to the ground, you who weakened and laid low the nations [O blasphemous, satanic king of Babylon.]"

Isaiah 14:12 (AMP)

This is how I believe the darkness came to earth in the pre-Adamic world. We know that the earth was here and was in darkness before God spoke light into being. I believe that Lucifer's rebellion against God brought darkness to the pre-Adamic earth. He was created as God's light source to give light to all of the first creation, which I will call the first heaven. This too was a perfect world until sin and darkness was found in Lucifer, and then he brought darkness to all the earth twice. "You were perfect in your ways from the day you were created, till iniquity (darkness) was found in you" (Ezekiel 28:15, NKJV). All of God's creation paid the price for this fall even as Adam's fall brought darkness to creation again. Not only did they pay the price for sin but all of creation and every human being since that time.

If Adam's sin could have caused the catastrophic collapse of the garden of Eden and its perfection, which I will call the second heaven, how much more could a powerful cherub like Lucifer not cause the fall of the first heaven? But now, God has given us a God-man named Jesus that did not fail God in His testing with the devil but took it all back from the enemy that stole it from Adam and is now going to restore it back to us in its original condition and better. I will call this new creation the third heaven, which is the kingdom of God on earth with His King on the throne and His overcomers (the bride) by His side ruling and reigning.

Scientists tell us that dinosaurs once roamed the earth millions of years ago, and they have found them in frozen tundra with green grass still in their stomachs. They say that the darkness came upon the earth so fast that it caused them all to die off very quickly. Science also says that an asteroid or something hit the earth that caused the sun's light to be blocked out for a long time, and all the vegetation died. My belief is that when Lucifer sinned, the light that was in him went out, and the earth became formless and void, which means "to be in darkness; misery, destruction, death, ignorance, sorrow, wickedness, and to lie waste and in desolation." Sounds like the effect of sin, does it not? Lucifer brought death and destruction to the earth even as man did when God destroyed the earth with Noah's flood. Had not Moses interceded for Israel at Mount Sinai, God would have destroyed them all for their rebellion against Him and raised up a new Israel from Moses. Sin has caused the fall of angels and man several times, but Jesus purchased us with His blood once and for all. Hallelujah!

You may say, "How could one angel be the light of the entire world?" Jesus said in Matthew 5:14, "You are the light of the world..." How can we who have such darkness in us be the light of the world? Because God the Father is so powerful that He can give His power to anyone to be the light of the world. Read what Jesus said He was: "I am the light of the world. He who follows me shall not walk in darkness, but have the light of life" (John 8:12, NKJV). Lucifer was called the morning star, but now Jesus is, and not only is He the morning star, He is the light of all creation: "I, Jesus, have sent my angel to testify to you these things in the churches. I am the root and the offspring of David, the bright and Morning Star" (Revelation 22:16, NKJV). God has set His eternal light in His place, and He shall never fall or be replaced by anyone because of sin or darkness being found in Him. Now, that is good news.

Jesus, the Light of the World

> Then God said, "Let there be light;" and there was light. And God saw the light, that it was good; and God divided the light from the darkness.
>
> Genesis 1:3–4 (NAS)

When God said, "Let there be light," it was because light was what the world needed most at the time of great darkness upon the earth. When most people read these verses in Genesis 1, they presume that God made the natural sun to give light to the earth. But that is not the case because verse 16 says, "Then God made two great lights: the greater light to rule the day, and the lesser light to rule the night. He made the stars also." The natural light was made on the third day and not on the first day as we might think. Why did God create two forms of light into existence, anyway? Because Lucifer not only left the world in physical darkness, but he also left it in spiritual darkness with his lies, deception, and fear.

Eve was deceived by the most cunning of all creatures with the power of persuasion to lie and deceive her into believing his words rather than God's. And what did Adam and Eve reap for their disobedience? Fear and a pack of lies. Jesus called the devil the Father of Lies, so where do you think he learned how to lie, deceive, and manipulate Eve and the rest of mankind? By deceiving all the other angels that he controlled in the first heaven, and God let him do it, just as Jesus let Judas steal the money from the bag and betray Him knowingly to bring about the Father's will in the end. God is working out His eternal purposes through all that is happening on planet earth, and yes, even in your life.

It is very important for us to know what kind of light was brought forth on the first day of creation for us to understand why Jesus had to come to save us from the darkness of deception. The greatest need for the earth and mankind is the light of God, which is the Word of truth. This is spiritual light that reveals Satan's darkness, lies, and deception that we cannot see or understand with our human intellect; our need is to have spiritual understanding (Colossians 1:9, NKJV). On the first day of creation, God revealed Himself as light to separate the darkness (deception) from the light (truth) and made a distinction between the two. Satan and sin represent darkness and deception, while God and light represents truth and freedom from sin.

The light of Jesus Christ is now in our heart if we have received Him, and we know that He is the light of the world; this is how John the Revelator saw Him: "His countenance was like the sun shining in its strength" (Revelation 1:16–17, NKJV). This is how Jesus was revealed on the first day of creation, the light, the Word of God, for He is the firstborn *over* all creation (Colossians 1:15, NKJV). This does not mean that Jesus was created, but that He was revealed as the light of God and was over all creation. Remember, God is light, and this is how He revealed Himself on the first day of creation. The name *God* in Genesis 1:1 is Elohiym, meaning "more than one." God revealed Himself in

Dan Luehrs

the first three verses of Genesis as the three in one. We see God the Father in Genesis 1:1, and then we see Him as the Spirit of God over the face of the deep in verse two, while we see Jesus as the light of the world in verse three. Now with this revelation at hand, that the Father revealed Jesus as light in the beginning, now read John 1:1–5 with the understanding of who and what He is in the Godhead:

> In the beginning [of creation] was the Word, and the Word was with God, and the Word was God. He was in the beginning with God. All things were made through Him, and without Him nothing was made that was made. In Him was life, and the life was the light of men.

Jesus is the Word of God that created all things in the beginning. However, this does not mean that the Bible is God. The Bible is God's way of revealing Himself as the light from generation to generation with the accuracy of the Hebrew and Greek languages. This is why the devil so opposes the Word of God from going out into print of the common people's language. The religious murdered many people in the 1500s that were printing the Bible in their language because they wanted to keep the people in darkness of their lies and deceptions.

Jesus is the light and life of every person; without His light, there is no life because the Father gave life unto Him. This is why there is no salvation in any other name but the name of Jesus. In order for us to come into the light of God, we must look into the face of Jesus as if we were to look at the sun to give light upon the earth. Because of Adam's fall, mankind was plunged into darkness and is in need of the light of God to enlighten our way back to Him to give us meaning to life. The eyes of our spiritual understanding is darkened without the knowledge of Christ and must be enlightened through knowing Jesus in a personal relationship, this brings light to us. "For it is the God who commanded light to shine out of darkness, who has shone in our hearts to give the light of the knowledge of the glory of God in the face of Jesus Christ" (2 Corinthians 4:6, NKJV). Man's heart was darkened with no spiritual knowledge or understanding about God and His ways because Satan has blinded mankind (2 Corinthians 4:4, NKJV). When Adam fell from his exulted place in God's kingdom, mankind was blinded to the true light of who Jesus Christ is, and we were without hope in the world. Only by us coming to Him through faith are all the veils of sin taken away from our spiritual eyes to see and understand God's ways through His Word and Spirit.

Time to Shine

Arise, shine; for your light has come. And the glory of the Lord is risen upon you. For behold, the darkness shall cover the earth, and deep darkness the people; but the Lord will arise over you, and His glory will be seen upon you. The Gentiles shall come to your light, and kings to the brightness of your rising.

Isaiah 60:1–3 (NKJV)

The Lord is saying to us at this time, "Arise, shine from the darkness and let the light of Christ [the knowledge of Him] come forth *from* you." We are now the light of God because the truth abides in us, even as we are living in the darkness of the world's understanding of who Jesus Christ is in us. There is no darkness so deep that the light cannot illuminate it.

And the light in the darkness is constantly shining. And the darkness did not overwhelm it.

John 1:5 (Wuest)

Dan Luehrs

It is not possible for the darkness to overwhelm the light and causing it to go out unless we allow it to. This comes about by our lack of time being spent with the Lord and asking Him to fill us with His spirit. We all have a need to stay filled with the oil of the Holy spirit burning in us. If we don't stay filled with Him, this will disqualify us from our high calling of shining forth His glory.

The Word of God is the light that created all things through the person of Jesus Christ, for He is the light. As we release the Word of God through our mouths, it will cause others to see the truth of Him and come to the light and knowledge of God's truth. Preaching the gospel is all about teaching the knowledge of God through the person of Jesus Christ.

> To give to His people the knowledge of salvation by the forgiveness of their sins, because of the tender mercy of our God, with which the Sunrise from on high shall visit us, to shine upon those who sit in darkness and the shadow of death, to guide our feet into the way of peace
>
> Luke 1:77–79 (NAS)

Jesus is the sunrise of knowledge that has come to give us the light (truth) of salvation that mankind desperately needs in this present dark hour. We are the ones that must ask and seek God to fill us with all spiritual wisdom and understanding in the knowledge of Jesus Christ. We will gain the experiential knowledge of God by our asking for it; it's not head knowledge that we need, but the experience of heart knowledge in the knowing of Jesus as our best friend. How do we get to know our best friend in this world so well? By spending time with him. We don't just read some history book or by what others have to say about them; we personally get to know them, and that is what God wants us to do.

Read these wonderful verses about us receiving the experiential knowledge of Jesus. God wants you to know Him.

That I may know Him and the power of His resurrection, and the fellowship of His sufferings, being conformed to His death.

Philippians 3:10 (NKJV)

That the God of our Lord Jesus Christ, the Father of glory, may give to you the spirit of wisdom and revelation in the knowledge of Him, the eyes of your understanding being enlightened; that you may know what is the hope of His calling, what are the riches of the glory of His inheritance in the saints.

Ephesians 1:17–18 (NKJV)

That you may walk worthy of the Lord, fully pleasing Him, being fruitful in every good work and increasing in the knowledge of God.

Colossians 1:10 (NKJV)

And have put on the new man who is renewed in knowledge according to the image of Him who created him.

Colossians 3:10 (NKJV)

For if, after they have escaped the pollutions of the world through the knowledge of the Lord and Savior Jesus Christ, they are again entangled in them and overcome, the latter end is worse for them than the beginning.

2 Peter 2:20 (NKJV)

Summary

There is nothing greater for us to gain in this world than a love for God's truth, the Word Himself. But He only gives this to people that are seeking and crying out to know Him more. I

Dan Luehrs

believe that the revelation of who Jesus is, is in us, and our high calling is to be like Him, then we will be like great lights in the earth and be given entire planets to enlighten with God's truth even as Lucifer was called to do. "Then the righteous will shine forth as the sun in the kingdom of their Father. He who has ears to hear, let him hear" (Matthew 13:43, NKJV). Peter writes even more clearly about these wonderful truths about our high calling to have the morning star shining through us in 2 Peter 1:19: "And we have the word of the prophets made more certain, and you will do well to pay attention to it, as to a light shining in a dark place, until the day dawns and the morning star rises in your hearts." Here is what he is saying: the Word of God, which was written through the prophets, is a shining light to enlighten our darkened heart. We must pay close attention to it so that our heart will be prepared for the return of Jesus, the bright morning star. The Word and Spirit of God were given to us to prepare us for His coming and our receiving of the morning star. Even as Lucifer was called of God to be a light-bringer, the morning star, so are we. We don't deserve it, but by the grace and mercy of God we get to partake of this wonderful high calling. No wonder Satan and his demons are so demented and hell-bent to stop us in our calling—because we are taking their place.

> And he who overcomes, and keeps my works until the end, to him I will give power over the nations. He shall rule them with a rod of iron; they shall be dashed to pieces like the potter's vessels' as I also have received from my Father; and I will give him the morning star. He who has an ear, let him hear what the Spirit says to the churches.
>
> Revelation 2:26–29 (NKJV)

The morning star has been given to us, my friend, so never, never give up on the promises of God.

The Marriage Supper of God

And he said to me, "Write, Blessed are those who are invited to the marriage supper of the Lamb." And he said to me, "These are true words of God."

Revelation 19:9 (NAS)

Just the sound of the words "The marriage supper of the Lamb" brings me great joy, excitement, and anticipation to my heart, as it should to every true believer. Weddings are times of joy and celebration, which includes a meal of one kind or another. We use food and drink to celebrate everything from birthdays, promotions, graduations, and of course, weddings. Food is not what we celebrate, and it does not matter what the food is, except that it tastes good. Depending on how wealthy the families are is what kind of food would be eaten at the celebration. I can tell you this for sure that Father God will give His Son the greatest banquet ever given to a son or a daughter's wedding, and money will not be an object whatsoever to Him. This wedding has been planned from the ages and will literally change heaven and earth from that day onward.

The cross and resurrection of Jesus Christ is the two greatest events in world history, and it changed the dates of the world from BC and AC. But what I tell you are true words of God: "Blessed are those who are invited to the marriage supper of the Lamb." I believe that the marriage of Jesus Christ to His bride will be the third greatest event in world history because it to will change the world as we know it from being unrighteous to righteous.

The Marriage

Let me tell you in a nutshell what I believe the Bible teaches us about this marriage. This union of Christ and His church is not so that they can live happily ever after on some cloud and have an eternity long honeymoon. Oh, no, it is a great mystery that is hidden in the pages of the Bible that we are to search out and know.

> Because we are members of His body. For this cause a man shall leave his father and mother, and shall cleave to his wife; and the two shall become one flesh. This mystery is great; but I am speaking with reference to Christ and the church.
>
> Ephesians 5:30–32 (NAS)

When we are married in our physical body, we become one with our spouse even though we are still living in separate bodies; yet we are still considered one because we are to become one in heart and purpose. So it is with Jesus and His bride. The coming of the Lord, or the return of Jesus Christ, is the marriage of the Lamb. This is when Jesus will change us into His likeness and glory. So that we can go to heaven? A thousand times no. It is so we can

Dan Luehrs

be with Him and fight in His triumphant return to destroy the enemy in the earth that lives in the flesh of mankind. The whole picture of this is found in Old Testament when God saved and called Israel out from under the hand of the Egyptians. Why did God call them? Just to live happily ever after in the wilderness? No. But to destroy the enemy of God!

One of God's names is, "The Lord of hosts." This means "the Lord of the armies." Israel was to be the army of God, which He would use to defeat the enemy within God's promised land. Israel was to be a worshipping army, or "Warshippers," if you will. Worship is not just people who sing and raise their hands to God, but that their life is caught up in serving God in all that they do. They are so in love with Jesus that He fills their every thought, and His presence surrounds them like a cloak of light to keep away the darkness that is overcoming many. "Keep yourselves in the love of God, waiting anxiously for the [marriage] mercy of our Lord Jesus Christ to eternal life" (Jude 21, NAS). Staying in love with Jesus will keep us until the wedding day. If you don't know how to, may I encourage you to spend lots of time with Him, for that is how we fell in love with our spouse, and that is how we will stay in love with Jesus.

The Army

Let us rejoice and be glad and give the glory to Him, for the marriage of the Lamb has come and His bride has made herself ready. And it was given to her to clothe herself in fine linen, bright and clean; for the fine linen is the righteous acts of the saints.

Revelation 19:7–8 (NAS)

God's army is clothed in white. Think of that. What army in the world would do such a thing? The world's armies dress in camouflage to hide from their enemy so that they will not be killed, but God's army dresses in the most brilliant white to be seen. These people will be able to be seen from miles away and still will not be scratched by one bullet from the enemy. The very light that shines from them is their armor.

> The night is almost gone, and the day is at hand. Let us therefore lay aside the deeds of darkness and put on the armor of light.
>
> Romans 13:12 (NAS)

Please understand the Bible is, not talking about a worldly army with guns and rockets, but one that is more powerful: "For the weapons of our warfare are not of the flesh, but divinely powerful for the destruction of fortresses" (2 Corinthians 10:4, NAS). The power we have is the Word, the blood, and the name of Jesus. The glory of God within is what causes us to shine like the sun to defeat the enemies of God, for nothing is greater in strength than Him.

Jesus promises us that if we will overcome in our lives, He will clothe us in His white garments (Revelation 3:5). The question herein lies: what is an overcomer? I believe it is a person that does not quit in his quest to know God. It does not matter what his life may look like on the outside, but that he has God's transformation in his heart. This is what matters, and only God can judge that.

> Therefore we do not lose heart, but though our outer man is decaying, yet our inner man is being renewed day by day. For momentary, light affliction is producing for us an eternal weight of glory far beyond all comparison, while we look not at the things which are seen, but at the things which are not seen; for the things which

Dan Luehrs

are seen are temporal, but the things which are not seen are eternal.

2 Corinthians 4:16–18 (NAS)

Jesus tells us in Revelation 3:18 to buy from Him white garments: "I advise you to buy from me gold refined by fire, that you may become rich, and white garments, that you may clothe yourself…" Jesus wants us to pay the price in following Him so that we may become like Him. Gold is symbolic to the nature of God, and that is what God wants us to become like; but in order for us to become pure gold, we must go through the fires of refining. This is paying the price. This is why we are told in Revelation 19:8, "And it was given to her to clothe herself in fine linen, bright and clean; for the fine linen is the righteous acts of the saints." It's not that we can earn anything from God by our good works, but that we continue on with the Lord in our trials and pay the price of following Him so that we are changed into His likeness. Staying faithful to God in our tribulation is considered as a righteous act, and it is through the trial we become overcomers.

It is written very clearly that the bride, the wife of the Lamb, is also His army of sons that will fight the great final battle of all times to defeat the enemy. When we start reading from chapter 19 *after* the marriage takes place to the end of the book of Revelation, we find that the devil and all the works of the flesh are finished for this period of time. By that I mean, the devil will be loosed from the pit for a short time once again to test the nations after a time of bliss without his evil presence in the earth. My friend, if you get nothing else from this writing, please understand this very clearly: chapter 19 is your calling and destiny to be a chosen and called son of God.

He who overcomes shall inherit these things, and I will be his God and he will be my son.

Revelation 21:7 (NAS)

We are the bride of Christ because we have intimacy with Him, and He is the lover of our soul. We are sons because we have overcome and are called to rule and reign over the nations with a rod of iron when the marriage takes place.

> And he who overcomes, and he who keeps my deeds until the end, to him I will give authority over the nations; and he (the overcomer) shall rule them with a rod of iron, as the vessels of the potter are broken to pieces, as I also have received authority from my Father.
>
> Revelation 2:26–27 (NAS)

Many of God's people are discouraged because they are not ministering to others like they would like to be. Or maybe they're at the end of their lives, and they have not fulfilled the vision that God has given them. Be encouraged that the last chapter has not yet been fulfilled. Your calling and destiny is found in Revelation chapter 19; this needs to be your focus: "His wife has made herself ready." We are being tested and tried with trials and tribulations to prepare us for our one true ministry with Him. This is when Jesus comes to slay the flesh of mankind with the sword of His mouth, which is the Word of God that we have become like. We will then have become like Him in all His glory and power: "Who will transform the body of our humble state into conformity with the body of His glory, by the exertion of the power that He has even to subject all things to Himself" (Philippians 3:21, NAS).

To be anointed and used of God is one of the greatest privileges a person can have in his lifetime. Out of all the experiences of my life, seeing others blessed and changed by the power of God flowing through me is a great wonder and joy that I could do over and over. Not just because I see people being blessed, but also because I can sense God working through me and I know that I could do nothing by my own power or calling. We may feel

Dan Luehrs

that God has more for us, and He does; those dreams, visions, and prophecies that have not been fulfilled in this lifetime will be fulfilled when Jesus returns in us if we do not give up hope and faith in the one who has called us. As it is written in Hebrews:

> And all these, having gained approval through their faith, did not receive what was promised, because God had provided something better for us, so that apart from us they should not be made perfect.
>
> Hebrews 11:39–40 (NAS)

The patriarchs of old did not see all the promises of God come to pass in their lifetime, and we may not either. But this I know that even when this life is over, God's promises are not because He is called faithful and true. What greater ministry could we ask for than to see the force of evil done away with in the earth? People say that they wish they would have been alive on the earth when Jesus ministered, but I tell you what is soon to come is going to be much greater and powerful because we will minister with Jesus throughout the earth and not just in the land of Israel.

The White Horse Ministry

> And the armies which are in heaven, clothed in fine linen, white and clean, were following Him on white horses.
>
> Revelation 19:14 (NAS)

These that are ready for His return are clothed in white because they were purified through the blood of Jesus. This is the second time this chapter speaks about their clothing being white or bright. I believe this also speaks about the light of the gospel and the glory of God that shines through them to defeat the enemy of darkness. Darkness cannot stand before the light/truth of God in them for this is the sword/Word of the spirit that comes out their mouths to slay the enemy. This is what God will use to kill sin in the flesh: His Word. God created the world and mankind as we know it with the spoken Word, and He will defeat the enemy through the same process: "And the rest were killed with the sword which came from the mouth of Him who sat upon the horse, and all the birds were filled with their flesh" (Revelation 19:21, NAS). I do not know how this will all take place, but we can see how God used Jonah greatly with the power to preach with such conviction that the whole city of Nineveh repented. Jesus said that Jonah was a sign of what is to come. (See Luke 11:29.) But somehow our preaching will be even greater than that of Jonah because sin or the flesh will be eaten by the demonic powers. I will say more on this later. Jesus Himself said, "Truly, truly, I say to you, he who believes in me, the works that I do shall he do also; and greater works than these shall he do; because I go to the Father" (John 14:12, NAS). Many in the church have looked for the greater works, but I am for certain that these greater works will come when the kingdom manifests itself through the Lord's people. For then all things will be restored: "And that He may send Jesus, the Christ appointed for you, whom heaven must receive until the period of restoration of all things about which God spoke by the mouth of His holy prophets from ancient time" (Acts 3:20–21, NAS). God is not just going to wave His hand and restore all things; no, His people will have the honor of doing that through His great power.

The white horse is symbolic, as are most things in the book of Revelation. For instance, a horse represents war, while a white horse is the color that a leader would ride before his troops to identify his rank. Back in John the apostle's day, the horse would be for speed and movement. That is what the white horse could very well mean in the book of Revelation that we are riding on. Not all Christians are going to be overcomers, and not all Christians will be riding white horses when Jesus returns. This is

Dan Luehrs

only for those who have overcome and passed the tests that He has allowed in their lives. These white horses are movements or ministries that Jesus Himself will work through to change the hearts of mankind and eventually the earth and all of God's creation back as it was before the fall and even better.

There have been a few ministries that have had such power that they shook nations where many people have been saved and delivered through their ministries. But somehow, sin took down many of these great men and women, and their ministries never came to its fullness that God had intended. Even Moses did not enter into the Promised Land because he sinned, and he could only look at it from a distance. May God help us to enter into all that He has for us. I believe that God would love to give us all power like Jesus had to raise the dead, heal the sick, and deliver mankind from death. But He knows better than to do that because there is no one on earth that could possibly handle such power without being overcome by the power of the flesh. But these people on the white horses will have been changed into Jesus' likeness, and the flesh will not be able to overtake them.

> For the anxious longing of the creation waits eagerly for the revealing of the sons of God.
>
> Romans 8:19 (NAS)

Why is creation waiting? To be delivered from death. Those on the white horses will deliver mankind from sin and death through power of God's Word.

> The last enemy that will be abolished is death. For He has put all things in subjection under His feet. But when He says, "All things are put in subjection," it is evident that He is excepted who put all things in subjection to Him.
>
> 1 Corinthians 15:26–27 (NAS)

The General

And I saw heaven opened; and behold, a white horse,
and He who sat upon it is called Faithful and True; and
in righteousness He judges and wages war.

Revelation 19:11 (NAS)

Jesus our general is the only faithful, true, and righteous one. He is a God of war against the power of the evil one and is the only one that can judge without partiality. He sees and understands all things and knows the motives of everything and everyone that He judges. He will deal out fair judgment to all, but not all judgment that He hands out will be bad, for there are many that have done well, and these will be rewarded with His likeness and glory. The duties of a general are to hand out promotions to the soldiers, and what greater promotion than to receive from our general, His likeness. When we come back with Him riding on a white horse, it's not because He felt sorry for us, but that we followed the Lamb wherever He led us. It was through the process of trials and tribulations that made us like unto Him: "For it was fitting for Him, for whom are all things, and through whom are all things, in bringing many sons to glory, to perfect the author of their salvation through sufferings" (Hebrews 2:10, NAS). If Jesus needed to suffer to be crowned with glory and honor, how much more us? God the Father has given Jesus a name above all names because He earned it through obedience to the Father. We also are called to die to the flesh upon our cross (trials) that we are carrying, and we are to live in the light of His glory each day. "And being found in appearance as a man, He humbled Himself by becoming obedient to the point of death, even death on a cross. Therefore also God highly exalted Him, and bestowed on Him the name which is above every name" (Philippians 2:8–9, NAS).

Dan Luehrs

The Rod of Iron and Sword

And from His mouth comes a sharp sword, so that with
it He may smite the nations; and He will rule them with
a rod of iron; and He treads the wine press of the fierce
wrath of God, the Almighty.

Revelation 19:15, NAS

If the teaching of the church is right about Jesus coming back to
kill most of mankind, then who would He be ruling over with
the sword and the rod? Jesus took the wrath of almighty God on
the cross for man, and now He has the right to rule and reign;
He does this through the power of His Word. If Jesus were to
kill mankind, He could not rule them. Both the rod of iron and
the sword in His mouth are alike and do the same thing; ruling over the hearts of mankind that need to be changed from
works of wickedness to being righteous: "But with righteousness
He will judge the poor, and decide with fairness for the afflicted
of the earth; and He will strike the earth with the rod of His
mouth, and with the breath of His lips [the Word] He will slay
the wicked" (Isaiah 11:4, NAS). His words created all, and it will in
the end rule and change the behavior of man. For now, God has
allowed things to go as they are but will soon change the outcome
of man, because if we keep going the way we are, we will destroy
the earth and all that is upon it. Right now, man is reaping what
we have sown, and we will suffer for it; but there are those who
have sown good seed, and those will also reap the benefit of their
works of righteousness.

Jesus said, "Man shall not live on bread alone, but on every
word that proceeds out of the mouth of God" (Matthew 4:4,
NAS). Notice the Bible does not say, "Every word that pro-
ceeded," but "Every word that *proceeds*." This means that God is
still speaking and will be in the future for man to hear and obey.

Scientists tell us that the universe is still growing at great speed. We can see when God puts things into motion with His Word, it continues to grow because His word is alive (Hebrews 4:12). It is the power of God's Word that keeps the earth and the universe and all that's in it working correctly because His Word holds it all together. "And He is the radiance of His glory and the exact representation of His nature, and upholds all things by the Word of His power ... " (Hebrews 1:3, NAS). If this is so, and it is, why do we not serve Him with godly fear and trembling? One day very soon, He is going to show His power and glory to all of mankind, and it will seem like a rod of iron and a sword that will slay the man of sin within all of us. His word will be fulfilled within all mankind. Hallelujah!

If people do not obey the Word of God, then they will not eat because judgment will come on them by having no rain to give them food. "And if the family of Egypt does not go up or enter, then no rain will fall on them; it will be the plague with which the LORD smites the nations who do not go up to celebrate the Feast of Booths" (Zechariah 14:18, NAS). This is one way that God will judge by the power of His Word.

If we are not using the sword of the spirit now to defeat the enemy of our souls in our personal life, how will we be able to use the Word later in ruling and reigning with Christ when He returns? We must understand that sin is not judged in our lives or the lives of others quickly, but when Jesus comes with the rod of iron and the sword, judgment unto correction will take place very quickly in the lives of people. We must pray for this now to take place in our lives so that we will be a clean and purified bride with no stains or blemish on our garment.

Have you ever been driving down the road and having cars passing you one right after the other, and then a highway patrol is seen, and then what happens? They all slow down and stay behind the officer because they know that if they speed, they will get a ticket, and it will cost them dearly. Do you see that

Dan Luehrs

when there is accountability, people straighten up really fast? So it will be when Jesus comes within His people with the rod of iron the nations will rage, but they will have no other choice but to comply to God's ways and rules. This is God's earth, and if man wants to live on earth when the kingdom comes, they will have no other way but God's way. So why not submit now and bring things in order in our own life to the sword (Word)?

The War

And I saw heaven opened; and behold, a white horse, and He who sat upon it is called Faithful and True; and in righteousness He judges and wages war.

Revelation 19:11 (NAS)

Do not think that I came to bring peace on the earth; I did not come to bring peace, but a sword.

Matthew 10:34 (NAS)

Many people think of Jesus as being sweet, meek, and mild, and He is. But I tell you He has another side; He is a man of war. For He is coming to make war with all that defies the Father's will on earth and for mankind. He is coming with a sword to defeat the enemy with the help of His bride. Who is the bride? Those who have become like Him so that they can rule and reign with Him over the enemy to bring lasting peace and righteousness to the earth.

The final battle that will be fought in this war will be against the man of sin that is working in all of us that no man has been able to defeat other than Jesus while in the flesh. Soon, the King of kings will come and fight for us and help us defeat the man of sin within each one of us. The battle within that each one of us fights every day will soon come to an end because our great

Warrior is on the march and nothing of the flesh can stand against Him.

When I read through the battles of the book of Joshua, I see how Joshua won over the enemy every time; he listened to God, and God fought their battles and destroyed the seven nations in the land of Canaan. It was that simple. Israel was outnumbered over and over in battle, and still they came through victorious because God was fighting for them. "Then the LORD said to Joshua, 'Do not be afraid because of them, for tomorrow at this time I will deliver all of them slain before Israel ...'" (Joshua 11:6, NAS). I believe that the book of Joshua is blueprint of how we are to fight the enemy and destroy the seven (complete) nations of sin that are living within us. The popular books and movies called *The Lord of the Rings* and *The Chronicles of Narnia* are prime examples of what God is going to do for us in these last days with the return of the King. No enemy will prevail against us because the time has come for the King to put all His enemies under our feet. When Israel and the people in these movies were outnumbered, they overcame because they would, not give in to their enemies, but withstood them and defeated them all.

The Supper of God

And he said to me, "Write, Blessed are those who are invited to the marriage supper of the Lamb." And he said to me, "These are true words of God."

Revelation 19:9 (NAS)

And I saw an angel standing in the sun; and he cried out with a loud voice, saying to all the birds which fly in mid-heaven, "Come, assemble for the great supper of God."

Revelation 19:17 (NAS)

Dan Luehrs

There is only one verse in the entire Bible that speaks about the marriage supper, yet the church has fabricated much foolishness about this great event—such as painting pictures of an endless table with the finest of china and the best of food and drink. Oh, and don't forget the chocolate cake for dessert.

We know that the book of Revelation is a book filled with many different symbols throughout, and this supper is just another symbol of what God is doing in the spirit realm. Just as the union of the bride to Jesus is to rise up a great army to fight and defeat the enemy, so is the supper of God; *it's for us to serve and not be served.* When we read through Revelation chapters 19 and 20, we see that when the marriage of the Lamb takes place, then the enemy of our soul is defeated and thrown into the bottomless pit: "And he laid hold of the dragon, the serpent of old, who is the devil and Satan, and bound him for a thousand years" (Revelation 20:2, NAS). This all happens because of the union of Christ to His bride. God could have done this at any point in history, but He did not because He wanted to share this great event with us, and it all happens in just a few short verses; but in reality, it may take many years to play out. Oh, what a great and mighty God we serve, for the enemy is no match for our God.

The Flesh Is Served Up

In order that you may eat the flesh of kings and the flesh of commanders and the flesh of mighty men and the flesh of horses and of those who sit on them and the flesh of all men, both free men and slaves, and small and great.

Revelation 19:18 (NAS)

And the rest were killed with the sword which came from the mouth of Him who sat upon the horse, and all the birds were filled with their flesh.

Revelation 19:21 (NAS)

These verses may sound gruesome and bloodthirsty, but remember that the sword (the Word) is coming out of Jesus' mouth, and I believe the mouths of all that are on the white horses to slay the man of sin that is within every person. The flesh or the carnal nature that has been plaguing mankind since the fall is about to be eaten by demons, or in other words, eliminated for good. Jesus did not come to destroy lives; He came to give it. When the disciples wanted to call down fire from heaven to slay the people that did not receive the Lord, what did Jesus say to them? "But He turned and rebuked them [and said], 'You do not know what kind of spirit you are of; for the Son of Man did not come to destroy men's lives, but to save them'" (Luke 9:55–56, NAS).

You still may be wondering at what will be the meat, which is to be served at the marriage supper. I will tell you plainly: the flesh will be served; not the flesh of mankind, but that which is of the sinful nature—the third part of mankind because we are three-part beings. Spirit, soul, and body, and it is the soul in man that the sin abides in, and the sin in the soul will be done away with. We do not have the power to kill sin completely in the soul because it always seems to rise up again when we think we have it defeated. But a day is soon coming when the Lord Jesus will come again and change these vile minds to the likeness of His. Then the sin-filled nature of man will be eaten by the demonic powers. Why? Because that is the curse that God has spoken upon them, and it cannot be changed or altered; they eat dust, and that is what we are made of: "And the LORD God said to the serpent, 'Because you have done this, cursed are you more than all cattle, and more than every beast of the field; on your belly shall you go, and dust shall you eat all the days of your life'" (Genesis

Dan Luehrs

3:14, NAS). We must understand that when we walk in the flesh, we are giving demonic powers the right to attack us because they see the earthly, fleshly, demonic nature of man, and they have this right to it because God gave it to them. James 3:15 says, "This wisdom is not that which comes down from above, but is earthly, natural, demonic." Our quest to die daily is, not just another Christian saying, but has real meaning today and especially when Jesus returns, or when we die physically the carnal nature will be done away with, and we thank God for that.

The End

It may be peculiar to entitle a chapter "The End." Teaching on the end times seems to be a hot button topic in the church that will usually draw crowds to hear the newest revelation on what the preacher believes God has shown them. In recent years, some Christian movements have come out with a different end-time scenario's than what has been typically taught in the church. But still, most mainstream Christians believe that the end pertains to a time when all people on the earth will be destroyed by the Antichrist while all the Christians being raptured out of the earth so that God can get rid of all the bad apples of mankind. While others believe that the earth will simply be annihilated by atomic bombs and life will cease to exist on earth as we know it because the earth will be inhabitable. But will there ever be an end to life on earth? No.

I believe that the words *the end* mean something much different than what we are taught to believe, and the words are much greater in depth than we can even imagine at this time. We know that the end is coming because Jesus said that there is an end coming in Matthew 10:22: "And you will be hated by all on account of my name, but it is the one who has endured to the end who will be saved." We can clearly see that an end is coming, but Jesus never said what the end is. But He did give us some clues of what the end is in Matthew 13:39: "The enemy that sowed them is the devil; the harvest is the end of the world; and the reapers are the angels" (KJV). Jesus said quite clearly that "the harvest" is the end. Again, church tradition teaches that the salvation of all the lost in the world is the harvest. They teach that there is one last person on earth that will be saved, then Jesus will come and rapture us away to heaven so that the Antichrist can kill all that he wants to in his reign of evil on earth. But they don't realize that God is waiting more patiently than they are for the harvest, which is the seed that He has planted in the hearts of His people when they were saved. The seed of Jesus is planted within every believer's heart so that it might grow up into His likeness and then be harvested.

> Be patient, therefore, brethren, until the coming of the Lord. Behold, the farmer [God] waits for the precious produce [the harvest of Christ's likeness] of the soil [us], being patient about it, until it gets the early and late rains.
>
> James 5:7 (NAS)

Jesus likened us to the four types of soil found in the book of Mark 4 where Jesus explains that we need to be good soil that will bring forth a one-hundred-fold harvest in us where the seed is planted. But it is only when the crop permits that it is harvested, for the seed must have an end to which it was sown. And that end is the harvest, the very likeness of the seed that was sown—Jesus. So it is with the sons of the kingdom that have been sown to grow into God's likeness; when the seed is fully grown, they are to be harvested.

Dan Luehrs

> And the field is the world; and as for the good seed, these are the sons of the kingdom; and the tares are the sons of the evil one.
>
> Matthew 13:38 (NAS)

> The children of the promise are counted as the seed.
>
> Romans 9:8 (NKJV)

The end is the harvest; that is the end of the seed that was sown in us. Our end is for us to receive God's eternal life—the crown of glory. When we have finished the course laid out for us, we will receive our full reward, the likeness of Jesus: "But now having been set free from sin, and having become slaves of God, you have your fruit to holiness, and the end, everlasting life" (Romans 6:22–23, NKJV). Eternal life is not just life that goes on and on, but it's God's life given to us so that we can give it away to others just as Jesus does. Jesus said that He is the eternal life because the Father had given it to Him even as He freely gives it to us on our harvest day. That will be the day that we will be given authority to rule and reign throughout eternity with Jesus.

Possessing the Kingdom

> But the saints of the Highest One will receive the kingdom and possess the kingdom forever, for all ages to come.
>
> Daniel 7:18 (NAS)

The book of Daniel is known as an end-time book. The phrase "The end" is spoken of much in it. Many people believe that it contains the pattern for how the end will come on earth and who are the main countries that God will use to bring about His desired end. Some of what they say is true, but much of it is not.

Most Bible teachers never—I mean, never—delve into the truth of the saints ruling because they simply do not comprehend, or maybe not even believe, that they are called to rule and reign with Jesus. The final decree has been written for all ages to come: "The saints of the Highest One will receive the kingdom." That kingdom is the Lord Jesus Christ in all His power and glory manifesting through His people. This cannot and will not change. Jesus said plainly in Luke 12:32: "Do not be afraid, little flock, for your Father has chosen gladly to give you the kingdom." Even though we are little in numbers and power, still the Father gladly gives us the kingdom with power and glory to do a work with Him, to turn the earth from being a sinful planet unto righteousness.

This will not come about in our timing or by our power, but in God's perfect time: "For the end is still to come at the appointed time" (Daniel 11:27, NAS). We will be given a crown (authority) to rule and reign with Jesus for overcoming in this life. However, this crown is not an earthly one that we wear upon our heads for others to see. No, it's a crown of God's authority that can be seen upon us as we go forth and minister in His glorious life to set mankind free from the bondage of sin and death. "That the creation itself also will be set free from its slavery to corruption into the freedom of the glory of the children of God" (Romans 8:21, NAS). These ministers of the true gospel will be the ones who will preach in the power of the truth to destroy the man of sin, which abides in every human being. Their words will deliver mankind from the power sin.

> And he [the man of sin] will speak out against the Most High and wear down the saints of the Highest One, and he will intend to make alterations in times and in law; and they will be given into his hand for a time, times, and half a time. But the court will sit for judgment, and his dominion will be taken away, annihilated and destroyed forever.
>
> Daniel 7:25–26 (NAS)

Dan Luehrs

The dominion of the man of sin in us will be taken away and destroyed forever. Hallelujah! No longer will the man of sin be able to control the human body through the sinful mind and heart because he will be no more. The Spirit of the living God will be inside of every person so that they will be yielding to Him and walking in true righteousness so that the kingdom of God will reign in and over every person upon the earth: "Then the kingdom and dominion, and the greatness of the kingdoms under the whole heaven, shall be given to the people, the saints of the Most High. His kingdom is an everlasting kingdom, and all dominions shall serve and obey Him" (Daniel 7:27, NKJV).

After this time of testing and trials in this life, we will be given dominion according to our walk with God and how closely we resembled His Son. Why would God give any part of His kingdom to someone that did not have the kingdoms best interest at hand? What president would appoint an ambassador to another country that he did not fully trust to represent the United States of America abroad in good faith? He wouldn't. Just as God would not appoint a person that He could not trust with the power of His kingdom. God is raising up sons that will have the likeness of His Son through their suffering so that they can be fully trusted with His power and glory to bring truth and ever lasting change to the earth. "In bringing many sons to glory [the kingdom], it was fitting that God, for whom and through whom everything exists, should make the author of their salvation perfect through suffering" (Hebrews 2:10, NIV).

Go Your Way

And he said, "Go your way, Daniel, for these words are concealed and sealed up until the end time."

Daniel 12:9 (NAS)

But as for you, go your way to the end; then you will enter into rest and rise again for your allotted portion at the end of the age.

Daniel 12:13 (NAS)

Be hopeful, my friend, for there is an end to all the madness that you are living in or that you will ever encounter in your lifetime, so don't despair. Daniel was clearly shown that what he was given would not be understood until we were at the end. Much has been revealed about the book of Daniel in our day, but I believe the end started when Jesus died on the cross, for that was the beginning of the end to the man of sin within us. Not until that time were we even able to war against the sin within us; we were simply sinners without hope of ever being freed from the power of sin. I believe the New Testament, and especially the book of Revelation, is the book that God has given us as a key to understanding the book of Daniel more clearly. But to put it simply, each of these books has an ending to the sin problem of man, and it all ends in God who created all things.

Many Christians would say, "Sin is not dead in me, for I was just tempted today." We must realize that just because we are tempted, that does not mean we are not saved or that the power of sin is not broken in us. When you received Jesus, the power of sin and death were broken in you. You still may say, "I am still warring against my flesh daily." That's good because it shows you that you are saved. If you were not saved, you wouldn't care less if you gave in to your sinful desires, but because you are saved, you care, and that is a true sign that you are indeed a child of God. Read Galatians 5:24: "And they that are Christ's have crucified the flesh with the affections [the sufferings] and lusts [strong desires]" (KJV). Do you see what this verse is saying to us? When we are warring against sin, we are suffering against the strong desires to sin from within. It is at this very time when we are crucifying the flesh, and it hurts to kill our own fleshly desires

Dan Luehrs

when they are dying within us. This is good for us because we are becoming overcomers in this life.

Here is another great verse for you to war against the flesh with: "Forasmuch then as Christ hath suffered for us in the flesh [or against the flesh], arm yourselves likewise with the same mind: for he that hath suffered in the flesh [against the sinful nature], hath ceased from sin" (1 Peter 4:1, KJV). Do you see it? Our suffering in the flesh is a true sign that we have stopped wanting to sin. God is allowing us to live in this sinful nature for Him to make us into the true nature of Christ, and that only comes about when we yield to Him in our time of temptation or testing. But before we can possess all that God has for us, we must allow God to possess us from within with the power of His Spirit. When we walk in the Spirit of God, we will not obey the strong desires of the flesh. (See Galatians 5:16.) By that, I mean, we are to receive our life from abiding in Jesus and from Him alone if we are going to make it through to the end. We can get our life from the Spirit of God if we are drawing from Him every day, and while we are at it, it might as well be every waking moment if we are going to make it to the end. We are going to get our life-sustaining power from something, so it might as well be from God.

God wants to give us life by knowing Him, for He has promised us His life if we will seek His will in all things: "So as to live the rest of the time in the flesh no longer for the lusts of men, but for the will of God" (1 Peter 4:2, NAS). Even as Jesus suffered against the flesh in the will of the Father, this verse clearly tells us that God wants us to suffer against the struggle of sin also. This is the will of God for us. This is how God is proving us to be found faithful in our trials; our faith then becomes more valuable than gold that perishes through the fires of life: "That the proof of your faith, being more precious than gold which is perishable, even though tested by fire, may be found to result in praise and glory and honor at the revelation of Jesus Christ" (1 Peter 1:7, NAS).

In 1 Peter 4:1, he encourages us to suffer with Jesus against sin, and that we are to arm ourselves with the same mind as He was so that we can make it through the assault from the enemy. He says in chapter 4:13, "We are shares or partaker of Christ's suffering." We must understand that when we are suffering against sin, we are being prepared by God to receive His glory, which is the very likeness of Jesus at His coming. But God uses the very thing that we hate: hardships, trials, and yes, even sin in our life that God has allowed so that we will be changed into His likeness. We claim that we are so weak against the sins of the flesh, and we are, but God has a master plan for us, and it is His will for us to stand against sin to make us strong. "But to the degree that you share the sufferings of Christ, keep on rejoicing; so that also at the revelation of His glory, you may rejoice with exultation" (1 Peter 4:13, NAS). We must keep our eyes on the joy set before us and not on our cross that we are called to bear. As we rejoice in faith at these things that try us, we are being changed trial by trial, so why not rejoice, for what are our alternatives, depression, the life of sin and death? No, we have been called to a much greater hope and joy set before us—His likeness.

> If ye then be risen with Christ, seek those things which are above, where Christ sitteth on the right hand of God.
>
> Colossians 3:1 (KJV)

Dan Luehrs

For more information about Dan and Marilyn and their ministry, or to invite them to minister in your area, visit their website at www.ChurchinHisPresence.org